THE SALT WAT

Easy Ways to Cut Dow
The hidden menace to your health—
what you can do about it!

THE SALT WATCHER'S GUIDE

Easy Ways to Cut Down on Salt and Sodium

by

Kathleen Mayes

THORSONS PUBLISHING GROUP
Wellingborough · New York

First published 1986

© KATHLEEN MAYES 1986

All rights reserved. No part of this book may be reproduced or utilized in any form or by any means, electronic or mechanical, including photocopying, recording or by any information storage and retrieval system, without permission in writing from the Publisher.

> British Library Cataloguing in Publication Data
>
> Mayes, Kathleen
>   The salt-watcher's guide: easy ways to cut down on salt and sodium.
>   I. Title
>   641.1'7   TX553.S65
>
> ISBN 0-7225-1242-2

Printed and bound in Great Britain

'The Panel recommends that the dietary intake of common salt should not be increased further and that consideration should be given to ways and means of decreasing it.

'We believe that the intake of salt in the United Kingdom diet (approximately 7-10g per day) is needlessly high. The salt content of many foods makes it difficult for the public to effect an immediate and substantial change in intake.

'Approximately 70 per cent of intake is salt present in food, much of it added during manufacture. Approximately 30 per cent is added at table or in cooking and this could be decreased immediately . . .

'Some feeding trials on normotensive and hypertensive adults, show small reductions in blood-pressure when salt intake is deliberately reduced, the effect being greater in those with high blood-pressure.'

Diet and Cardiovascular Disease
Committee on Medical Aspects of Food Policy
Report of the Panel on Diet in Relation to
Cardiovascular Disease
D.H.S.S. (1984) H.M.S.O.

Author's Note

The use of brand names in this publication is for identification only and does not imply endorsement or otherwise by the author. The sodium values in this book have generally been derived from 'The *Composition of Foods*' (McCance and Widdowson) 4th Edition by A. A. Paul and D. A. T. Southgate of the Medical Research Council, published by Her Majesty's Stationery Office, 1978. Further sodium figures have been provided by '*The Sodium Content of your Food*' (U.S. Department of Agriculture, Home & Garden Bulletin No. 233) or directly from food manufacturers. Where there is a discrepancy, an average figure has been given. Processing practices and formulas may vary from time to time, and the nutrients in fruits and vegetables can vary according to soils in various parts of the country, or from season to season, but the sodium values are those currently available.

Contents

	Page
Foreword by Professor John Catford	11
Introduction	13

Chapter
1. What's It All About? — 21
2. What Can We Do About It? — 33
3. An A-to-Z Guide to Cutting Salt and Sodium — 45
4. Where Are You Going? — 55
5. What Are You Drinking? — 61
6. What's in the Medicine Cabinet? — 67
7. Software for Salt-Watchers — 71
   Appendix I: The Sodium Content of Your Food — 79
   Appendix II: Herb and Spice Chart — 113
   Appendix III: Low-Sodium Food Manufacturers — 121
   Index — 125

Foreword

Since time immemorial, we have known that good health depends on a sound diet. Few people would elect to eat unwholesome food if they were completely free to choose. But a genuinely free choice depends on whether people know what foods are thought to be healthy, whether people can easily distinguish healthy foods from others and whether healthy foods are widely available at prices people can afford. Unlike many other countries, we, unfortunately, still have a long way to go in Britain to achieve these essential prerequisites for a healthy diet.

This book is for those who wish to moderate the excessive quantity of sodium currently present in the British diet, and particularly for those who have been advised by their doctor to reduce dietary sodium for specific health reasons. The rationale for lowering sodium and sodium chloride (common table salt) in our food centres round the importance of preventing and controlling raised blood-pressure, which is a major cause of heart disease and stroke. Hypertension has now reached epidemic proportions — equal in scale to the serious infectious diseases of the last century like tuberculosis, cholera and smallpox. As a nation we responded energetically to these former scourges, often with less than ideal information. We must now do the same for hypertension. As one of a number of contributions, there is an urgent need not only to accept that we probably eat too much sodium for our own good, but also to take action to lower dietary intake.

Like all things in life, we need to be sensible and balanced in our approach. Very drastic reductions in sodium intake, although extremely difficult to achieve, could be harmful. Also sodium is not the only thing in which we are interested, in terms of promoting healthy nutrition. As a nation we also eat too much fat, particularly animal fat, sugary foods and too little fibre. There is also increasing concern about the widespread use of food additives and preservatives. An improvement in our diet in these areas — including sodium — could well result in an important reduction in the excessively high levels of heart disease, cancer, diabetes, tooth decay and obesity that we experience in Britain more commonly than many other developed countries.

The Salt-Watcher's Guide is an important contribution to the quest for a healthy diet. It uniquely bridges the gap between what the medical evidence indicates is good for our health and what practical action ordinary people can take to improve their own health and that of their families.

Professor John Catford
Director, Welsh Heart Programme

Introduction

Do you know how much salt you have in a day? Just think about what you eat in the ordinary way: you may have some cornflakes and milk for breakfast, a beer at midday with a Ploughman's (some good Cheshire cheese, bread and pickles on the side), a few crisps or nuts and a soft drink while waiting for dinner — 'a nice bit of ham' from the supermarket with tinned peas and a salad with dressing, a slice of cake for a sweet. Before you go to bed you might take a laxative or an antacid, and brush your teeth. Do you know how much sodium is in your cornflakes and milk? In the other food? Even in the laxative and toothpaste? You may not salt your food at the table, but you're eating more sodium than you realize, and probably far more than you should have.

This book is for *everyone* — not just for those who have already been warned by their doctors to cut out salt and sodium, as the evidence is now mounting that medical problems arise as our intake of salt increases.

In recent years we've become over-dependent on salt in food processing, eating far more than our systems are designed to cope with. The mechanisms in our bodies evolved in the Stone Age at a time when sodium (as in meats) was generally scarce, and when potassium (as in fruits and vegetables) was abundant. Our kidneys are designed to retain sodium and eliminate potassium. The diet we are eating today, however, is exactly the reverse of this, with the result that extra sodium accumulates in the fluids of the body, attracting water to maintain the equilibrium. The volume of blood appears to increase, raising blood-pressure and the workload on the heart.

Sodium comes into our diet in many ways, although common table salt is by far the major source. Much of the sodium in foods is put there by nature, as it occurs in all parts of plants and animals; but it can come from many other sources including ingredients added to foods — like bicarbonate of soda, monosodium glutamate, the flavour enhancer, and sodium ascorbate in vitamin C. Once sodium is in your body and circulating in the blood, your body can't distinguish where the sodium came from, but out of all the food items you can buy today in a supermarket, practically every one contains sodium to a certain degree.

As a rule of thumb, about a third of sodium may come from food in its natural state, a third was put in by a food-processing firm, and the remaining third gets added by you at home or in a restaurant. The food manufacturer puts it in for many purposes some of which are essential for safely preserving food.

But health experts are saying we generally eat up to *twenty times* more salt than our bodies need.

An Essential Nutrient

Salt is an essential nutrient to life and the normal functioning of your body, but most people's needs can be met without extra amounts in food. In a healthy body, salt reaches the intestines and then gets absorbed into the bloodstream, added to the blood plasma and body fluids. Your body separates the salt into sodium and chloride components — both necessary to maintain life — uses what it needs and eliminates the remainder. Put simply, the hormone *renin* in your kidneys normally regulates the balance of sodium in your body, essential for maintaining blood-pressure. Sodium attracts water into the blood-vessels, keeping the proper blood volume and the pressure within the blood-vessels more or less constant. Sodium is also intimately involved in the production of hormones regulating blood-pressure, and adjusting the acid-alkaline balance in your body, work done largely by the kidneys.

Each individual requires varying amounts of salt, according to size, age and activities: you can lose a lot through perspiration in hot weather, when you have a strenuous athletic programme or when you work physically hard. But nowadays people probably don't perspire as much as they used to, because they do not work so hard physically and are often in air-conditioned workplaces.

The trouble is that some people appear sensitive to excess sodium, resulting in health problems, while some are not. It is difficult to predict who will be susceptible, so the best course is for everyone to lower his or her intake of salt and sodium before trouble develops.

Let's consider some of the medical problems connected with too much sodium:

Hypertension: Since 1904 it's been suspected that there was a relationship between salt and high blood-pressure, and studies now show that hypertension develops several times more often among heavy salt users than among those who do not salt their food. Hypertension, which has been described as a 'silent killer' because there are few outward signs, is one of the leading health problems of today's Western world, widespread in the UK, where it is an important cause of at least a third of premature heart attacks and strokes. Someone dies every *three minutes* from heart disease! In 1980, according to the Office of Population Censuses and Surveys, 48 per cent of men and 41 per cent of women suffered premature death due to circulatory disease (chiefly heart attacks and strokes) — the biggest single cause of death before the age of 75. Recent reports show that coronary heart disease alone costs the National Health Service more than £245 million in hospital services. Drugs for treating heart disease cost the National Health Service over £215 million per annum, and over £90 million per annum for the treatment of hypertension. Up to a *quarter* of Britain's drug expenses are connected with the prevention and control of coronary heart disease. It's a heavy cost to the country.

But we *shouldn't* assume or expect that as we age we will have higher blood-pressure in our later years. Hypertension is *not* an inevitable part of growing older. Much of the pain, problems and expense could be reduced, with a decrease in the amount of salt and sodium you're presently eating.

Do you know if you have high blood-pressure? As your heart

pumps blood through your arteries, the push of this blood on the artery walls determines the amount of pressure. The artery walls are elastic, stretching and contracting to take the ups and downs of blood-pressure. Each time the heart contracts (or beats), the pressure in your arteries increases; then when the heart relaxes between beats, the blood-pressure goes down. So there is an 'upper' (or *systolic*) reading and 'lower' (or *diastolic*) reading, both pressures being measured when you are examined by your doctor. When your pressure is recorded, the higher number is written first, then the lower: an example would be 120/80 — the 120 is the systolic pressure and the 80 is the diastolic pressure.

But there's no blood-pressure reading that is 'normal' for everyone. Your age, sex and overall health help your doctor determine what is 'normal' and healthy for you. Blood-pressure not only varies among people but it can vary in the same person at different times: during sleep, during exertion or when you're excited — even the stress of visiting a doctor's surgery may temporarily raise blood-pressure, which is why a person with a high reading may need to have it rechecked several times.

High blood-pressure makes your heart pump harder, with the arteries less elastic, so eventually your heart may enlarge, then weaken, and stop pumping effectively.

Stroke: Another complication of untreated hypertension is stroke (or haemorrhage of a brain blood-vessel). When blood-pressure is high, exerting too much force when passing through the arteries, this excess force may weaken an artery in the brain. If blood-pressure remains too high, the weakened artery may rupture, causing a cerebral haemorrhage. High blood-pressure is a major cause of stroke.

Kidney failure: Hypertension can also affect the kidneys, and when the blood-vessels to these organs are constricted, they can no longer perform their task of clearing wastes from the bloodstream.

It's well documented that hypertension is apt to run in certain families, so when your doctor checks your blood-pressure, tell him if you have any close relatives with heart problems. Researchers have found elevated blood-pressure readings even in youngsters in these vulnerable families. Twice as many black people suffer as whites, probably because they may have a system in their bodies that tends to retain greater amounts of salt and to excrete less sodium.

No one should embark on a drastic diet of severe sodium-restriction without consulting a physician, as too little sodium can lead to muscle cramps, lethargy and general weakness. But if your doctor considers you have mild hypertension, in many cases this could be controlled wholly or partly by a reduction in the amount of salt and sodium you eat.

If your doctor says you have high blood-pressure, follow his directions: take your medicine, keep your weight down, reduce your consumption of fats, take exercise, cut out smoking, and try to reduce stress and anxiety in your life; and very often when medication is supplemented by a low-sodium diet, it's possible to reduce the amount of drugs needed. Some people suffer side effects from anti-hypertensive medication, if it's on a long-term or life-long basis, causing problems of impotence or depression — how much easier to control your blood-pressure by eating less salt and sodium?

Oedema: Some women have puffiness and swelling of tissues — a condition that doctors refer to as oedema. The bloating of face, ankles, wrists and hands, and swollen breasts, can be a common problem among women as a premenstrual symptom, a problem during pregnancy or a symptom of menopause. It's estimated that 40 per cent of all women suffer PMS sometime in their lives, and for 10 per cent of sufferers, it's severe enough to disrupt their personal lives and jobs.

Oedema, or water retention, can occur for many different reasons: when the body's water-regulating system is working incorrectly, kidney or liver disease, heart or circulatory problems, hormone imbalance, allergies — or too much sodium in the diet. Premenstrual fluid retention is connected with the level of oestrogen in the second half of the menstrual cycle. Oestrogen and progesterone hormones are both a natural part of a woman's cycle, but oestrogen is also a powerful sodium-retaining hormone. The more oestrogen a woman produces, the more fluid she may retain. And if contraceptive pills containing only oestrogen are used, or if a woman is having Oestrogen Replacement Therapy during or after menopause, oedema is often a side-effect.

Diuretics that induce your body to release water may be prescribed by your doctor, but they can be habit-forming. The kidneys are forced to work overtime, flushing out potassium and causing a loss of important minerals like calcium along with the increase in urine, resulting in a disturbance of the body's necessary balance between sodium and potassium — thus causing even more severe swelling when diuretics are stopped.

With the natural increase in oestrogen levels during pregnancy, swollen ankles are a common problem. Towards the end of pregnancy, six or more quarts (litres) of water are often retained: half cushions the growing foetus, with the rest distributed in the mother's blood, breasts and uterus. Feet and legs often swell the most because the growing uterus compresses the large veins that return blood to the heart from the lower extremities.

To combat bloating, try lying down for a few minutes during the day, with your feet and legs raised. Studies have shown that women can excrete more water after lying down, compared to an upright position. Carbohydrates should be reduced — sugary, sweet foods and starchy items — and there should be an increase in naturally diuretic, water-releasing foods like cucumber, parsley, watercress, beets, asparagus, strawberries, apples, grapes and pineapple. But most important is a reduction in your sodium intake, six or seven days immediately before your menstrual period.

Gastric cancers: Research studies are not conclusive, but the consumption of large amounts of salt-cured and salt-pickled foods may be related to cancers of the stomach and oesophagus, so reducing intake of salty foods may help avoid these problems.

But don't wait to become another addition to Britain's statistics. Many of the foregoing medical conditions don't have to happen in the first place.

Are *you* a saltaholic? Eating salt is a habit, usually learned in childhood, and a habit that can be 'unlearned' by re-educating your taste-buds.

What makes you salt your food? Have you ever stopped to think about it? Do you automatically reach for the salt-cellar when you sit down at the dinner-table? Do you taste the food first, and *still* shake the salt on? Would you eat salt if it cost you £1 an ounce? Have you ever *really tasted* the true flavour of a dish without that blanket of salt? And when you're in the kitchen, do you use the salt because mother did it that way? And you've always done it like that? Because all recipes and cookery books say 'cook in salted water'? Think about it a minute . . . Do you know the true taste of vegetables, especially those young fresh vegetables from the garden? The flavour doesn't need a mask of salt. Maybe a little accent with a herb or two or a squeeze of lemon. Hold back the salt! New worlds await you when your taste-buds wake up to different sensations. Youngsters don't need salted food. Don't start them on the salt habit and they'll never need it.

How much salt do *you* add to your food? Try this test: cover a plate with greaseproof paper. Now salt the plate as if it contained food. Collect the salt and measure it. If you've used about one-eighth of a teaspoon, that amounts to 250 mg of sodium.

By automatically sprinkling salt on everything you eat, you could have 10 or more extra pounds of water retained in your body; a low-salt diet may result in weight loss as this water is released. But if you're obese, don't expect to lose weight permanently this way: regular exercise is still important, as fatty tissues retain more water than muscle, and a reduction in calories is the only way to lose excess poundage.

And don't cut back on the amount of water you drink, to counteract water-retention; doctors still recommend four to six glasses a day.

The change-over from your usual meals to a reduced-sodium style won't take place in a single day, no one said it was going to be easy, and most meals may taste bland at first.

But, you may argue, 'I hardly ever put salt on my food at the dinner-table.' And this is where you can be deceived, because only a portion of the salt in your diet comes from the amount you consciously add to food, and the remainder is derived from manufactured processed foods.

Today, in the Western world, we enjoy a super-abundance of high-quality fresh fruits, vegetables and meats, but much of this vast production goes to be processed, canned, preserved in brines, made into 'convenience' and take-away foods. There has also been a big increase in the consumption of snack foods in recent years, like crisps and nuts which are highly-salted.

We're paying a price for this convenience, with the health of the people, and a high rate of premature death. Processed 'convenience' foods may offer short cuts in the kitchen, but the high salt and sodium content in your diet could be cutting short your life!

Let's prevent heart attacks and strokes. Let's say *down* with high blood-pressure! Cut the salt! Cut the sodium!

BE A SALT-WATCHER!

1
What's It All About?

Let's clear up any confusion: what exactly is salt, and what is this stuff called sodium? How much are we supposed to have, and how much would be too much?

What is Salt?

Common salt is white or colourless; a crystalline compound of sodium and chlorine, chemically known as NaCl. A teaspoon of table salt contains about 40 per cent sodium, 60 per cent chlorine, by weight. Salt can be in a solid form, as in halite, or in a solution, such as brine. There's plenty of salt in nature, with life starting in the salty sea. The development of human life needs the salty waters of the womb. There is the same salinity in your blood today as in the ocean. So salt is found in sea-water, in small amounts in fresh water, and in all animal fluids. Salt or sodium is with us everywhere — on the land, in the oceans and in our bodies. A man weighing 11 stone (70 kilos) has about 1¼ oz (35g) of sodium in his body, which amounts to about 3 oz (75g) of salt.

Some History

For millions of years, primitive man ate a vegetarian diet and did not consume much salt, apart from the small amounts naturally found in fruits, berries and roots. But when our ancestors became herdsmen they had to look for salt deposits for their animals, since flocks and herds that do not eat meat need a supply of salt. Salt is only found in certain parts of the world, and underground deposits of salt were beyond reach of ancient men, so it was a precious commodity. Tribes waged war, civilizations grew or diminished, depending on their access to salt. Salt was carried across African and Asian deserts by ancient caravans, with an old route leading from Morocco southwards across the Sahara to Timbuktu; and Herodotus describes another route uniting the salt oases of the Libyan desert. Ships with cargoes of salt crossed the Mediterranean and Aegean seas from Egypt to Greece.

Rome's major highway was the Via Salaria (Salt Road) along which marched soldiers and merchants driving oxcarts full of the crystals from the salt pans at Ostia on the west coast. Roman soldiers received part of their wages in salt (Latin: *salarium argentum* hence our word 'salary'). And a soldier's pay was cut if he 'was not worth his salt', a phrase that was used because Greeks and Romans frequently bought slaves with salt. Salt was offered to the gods in the temples, and grains of salt were put on babies' lips in an ancient Roman rite of purification.

In the sixth century, as tribes roamed to distant places and the need arose for food to be preserved, Moorish merchants routinely traded salt ounce for ounce with gold. In 1295, Marco Polo brought back tales to the Doge of Venice of the tremendous value of salt-coins in Tibet, stamped with the seal of the great Khan. Cakes of salt were used as money in parts of central Africa (and even until early this century salt could still be used to purchase a bride).

In medieval times, the holiness of salt changed to a feeling of superstition, so when salt was spilled, a small amount had to be thrown over the left shoulder to forestall doom and placate the evil spirits that supposedly lurked there. In 'The Last Supper', painted by Leonardo da Vinci, an upset salt-cellar is in front of Judas Iscariot as a bad omen.

Social prominence in the Middle Ages was marked at banquets in relation to the large central salt-cellar at the table, with worthy guests and their host 'above the salt', — those below were of a lesser status and of little consequence.

Governments exerted power by imposing salt taxes: in France, for hundreds of years salt could only be bought from royal stockpiles, and the *gabelle*, the hated high tax on salt during Louis XVI's reign, was one of the injustices that triggered the French Revolution. In 1805 in Britain, the tax on salt was £30 per ton, until salt taxes were finally abolished in 1825. As recently as 1930, Indians protested the high tax on salt imposed by the British, with Mahatma Gandhi leading many of his followers on a pilgrimage to the seashore to make their own salt illegally.

Salt has always had an important place in the history of man.

Where is Salt Found?

Ancient seas once covered the earth, and when these receded or evaporated, the salt deposits remained, leaving sufficient salt to supply man's needs for thousands of years to come. In Louisiana where large deposits occur, salt is mined from domes reaching 50,000 feet deep into the earth. Salt is also produced from evaporative pans in Brittany, France, and in Western Australia and at Lake Grassmere on the South Island of New Zealand.

In Britain the salt industry is centred in Middlewich, Cheshire (known to the Romans as *Salinae*), where 1½ million tons of white salt is produced from underground brine and sea salt. A further 1½ million tons of rock salt is mined, used mostly to de-ice the roads.

The main method used in Britain for producing salt is through evaporating saturated brine, by 'solution mining' of deposits. In recent years, sea salt and rock salt have become popular, but these types of salt are identical to common salt, although they could have additional trace amounts of minerals.

How is Salt Used?

Of that 1½ million tons of white salt:
    750,000 tons goes to the chemical industry;
    200,000 tons is for human consumption;
    60-70,000 tons is for animal feeds;
    60,000 tons is for water-softening.
And of the 200,000 tons for human consumption:
    80-100,000 tons goes to food manufacturers;

100-120,000 tons is for domestic use (table salt);
of which:
10,000 tons is used on pavements.

Salt is put to a variety of uses: in preserving foods; in seasonings; and in manufacturing chemicals, for producing hundreds of items — soaps, synthetic fabrics, detergents, plastics, paper and synthetic rubber.

A hundred years ago there were many small companies producing, purifying and packing salt for sale, but now 96 per cent of the processing in the industry is run by ICI and British Salt, although salt may appear under many different labels.

About 70 per cent of the packeting of salt is done by Rank Hovis McDougall (RHM Foods) under their main labels of *Saxa* and *Cerebos*, with *Sifta* in the Midlands, and the private labels for the supermarket and grocery chains.

Each household in Britain buys an average of 6 lb (2.7 kilos) a year, worth about £1 (at 1985 prices).

Apart from table salt, there are many other types of salt in general use today:

Canning Salt	Plain evaporated salt with no additives.
De-icing Salt	Salt, either in rock or solar form, used to melt ice and snow on roads in winter.
Enriched Baker's Salt	Salt that contains thiamine, riboflavin, niacin and iron and is used in commercial baking.
Evaporated Salt	Salt produced by open pan or vacuum pan evaporation of brine under conditions designed to control crystal size and purity.

Flour Salt	A superfine grade of salt for use in cake mixes and other commercial baking.
Ice-cream Salt	Usually rock salt; used to enhance the freezing process in making ice-cream.
Iodized Salt	Salt that has a minute amount of potassium iodide added as a preventive against goitre.
Kosher Salt	A coarse evaporated salt produced under conditions approved by the Orthodox Jewish Faith for use in Kosher foods.
Popcorn Salt	Fine particles of evaporated salt, used in seasoning popcorn.
Pretzel Salt	A coarse salt used in making pretzels.
Rock Salt	A mineral halite (sodium chloride) occurring in the form of rock masses and beds.
Sea Salt	Salt produced from sea-water; same as solar salt.
Solar Salt	Salt produced by evaporation of sea, salt lake or underground saline waters by sun and wind in shallow ponds.
Trace Mineralized Salt	Salt in either loose, brick or 50 lb (23 kilos) block form that has minute amounts of trace minerals added, used in livestock feeding.

> **Water Softener Salt**   High quality, either rock, solar or compressed evaporated in pellet or block form, used to regenerate water-softening systems.
>
> (*Reproduced by kind permission of the U.S. Salt Institute*)

What is Sodium?

Sodium is a mineral that is essential to life and needed for good health. It comes naturally in most of the foods we eat, although the amount varies: most fruits contain little sodium; vegetables vary from low-count to a considerable quantity; poultry, fish, meat, milk and cheese are fairly high in sodium. And sodium is present in our water supplies, with the amount depending on geographical location.

Sodium is measured in milligrams, usually shortened to 'mg'. Let's look at this little table for some comparisons:

> 1 oz of salt equals about 28,000mg (28 grams).
> 1 level teaspoon salt weighs about 6,000mg.
> 1 level teaspoon salt contains about 2,000mg sodium.

How is Sodium Used?

Apart from the 2000 milligrams of sodium found in a teaspoon of table salt, and the amounts of sodium naturally present in food, there are many other ways by which sodium is added to food by processors and manufacturers.

- Preserved *meats* (tinned, salted, pickled, smoked) are especially high in sodium: hams, bacons, sausages, luncheon meats, black pudding, corned beef, dried chipped beef; also pork pies, steak and kidney pies, Cornish pasties, commercial beefburgers.
- Smoked, brined, or canned *fish* can be high-sodium: tuna fish,

smoked herrings, kippers; anchovies, tinned salmon, sardines, scallops, shrimps and prawns, crab, fish pastes.
- Tinned and dehydrated *soups* are high in sodium.
- Some *cheeses* are high in sodium: blue, Roquefort, Féta, cottage cheese and processed cheese.

Varieties of cheese can be numbered in their hundreds, but basically the process for making them is the same, in that the milk-curds are salted during preparation. Wheels of cheese are often stored in cool cellars, spread with layers of salt or soaked for days in salty brines, put on shelves to be sprinkled with fresh salt. Roquefort cheeses are salted regularly as they age in the famous caves of Combalou. Beneath the pastures surrounding Chester there are salt springs, with the result that the milk has a salinity that is imparted to the cheese from that region. Cheese can also be salted with so-called smoked salt.

Most of us know how salty some foods can be, such as anchovies, kippers, green olives, pickles and salted crisps. But a lot of the salt and sodium we eat is concealed in foods we wouldn't think of as containing salt — *bread* and *breakfast cereals*, *puddings* and *cake mixes*. And although most raw fresh vegetables are low in sodium to start with, they may become high-sodium after commercial processing and canning.

Look at some of the sodium compounds that are being used to process foods:

Monosodium glutamate	To enhance flavour and to season.
Sodium alginate	Used in ice-cream and milk drinks to prevent separation.
Sodium benzoate	For preserving sauces, salad creams and pickles.
Sodium bicarbonate (bicarbonate of soda)	To improve the texture in breads; putting the fizz in drinks and laxatives.

Sodium bicarbonate and sodium pyrophosphate (baking powder)	For leavening breads and cakes.
Sodium carbonate, monohydrate	As a buffer to keep acid-alkali balance.
Sodium citrate	Flavouring.
Sodium hexametaphosphate, sodium tripolyphosphate	For improving moisture retention, and the colour and texture in processed meats.
Sodium nitrite (nitrate)	To prevent growth of dangerous microbes and to improve the colour in cured meats.
Sodium propionate	For preserving breads and cakes, and in pasteurized cheese.
Sodium saccharin	For non-caloric sweetening.
Sodium silico aluminate	Used in table salt to keep it flowing freely.
Sodium sulphite	For preserving some dried fruits.

Sodium-based Additives

E numbers are used to represent specific food additives on food labels. Here is a list of additives which are sodium-based, with their respective E number:

E201	sodium sorbate
E211	sodium benzoate
E221	sodium sulphite
E222	sodium hydrogen sulphite
E223	sodium metabisulphite
E237	sodium formate
E250	sodium nitrite
E251	sodium nitrate
E262	sodium hydrogen diacetate
E281	sodium propionate
E301	sodium-L-ascorbate
E325	sodium lactate
E331	sodium dihydrogen citrate
E331	diSodium citrate
E331	triSodium citrate
E335	sodium tartrate
E339(a)	sodium dihydrogen orthophosphate
E339(b)	diSodium hydrogen orthophosphate
E339(c)	triSodium orthophosphate
E401	sodium alginate
E450(a)	diSodium dihydrogen diphosphate
E450(a)	tetraSodium diphosphate
E450(a)	triSodium diphosphate
E450(b)	pentaSodium triphosphate
E450(c)	sodium polyphosphates
E466	carboxymethylcellulose, sodium salt
E470	sodium, potassium and calcium salts of fatty acids
E481	sodium stearoyl-2-lactylate

How Much is Enough?

Research continues on the effects of too much or too little sodium and opinions vary. Many people need only 200 to 220mg per day to survive, to maintain salt balance and to produce the necessary body fluids (saliva, digestive juices, perspiration, etc.) But such severe restriction is not suggested unless under medical supervision.

The Food and Nutrition Board of the National Academy of Sciences, National Research Council in Washington has a list of Recommended Daily Dietary Allowances of nutrients found in a variety of common foods, and for normal healthy people they suggest the following would be safe and adequate:

Age	**Milligrams of sodium per day**
0 to 6 months	150
6 months to 1 year	250 to 750
1 year to 3 years	325 to 975
4 years to 6 years	450 to 1350
7 years to 10 years	600 to 1800
11 plus	900 to 2700
Adult	1100 to 3300

Two World Health Organization Expert Committees on the Prevention of Coronary Heart Disease and Hypertension recommended in 1982 and 1983 that consumption of salt be limited to 5 grams per day (2000mg of sodium).

And in Britain, the Health Education Council stated in February 1983 that, whereas the average person eats about 12 grams of salt every day (about 2½ teaspoons, or about 5000mg of sodium), the Council recommended cutting your total intake down to about 9 grams a day (less than 2 teaspoonsful, or about 3800mg of sodium). A reduction *of at least 10 per cent* could be very good for you and (in their words) 'It certainly won't do you any harm'. More recently, in 1984, the Department of Health Committee on Food Policy recommended that consideration be given to ways and means of reducing salt intake in the United Kingdom.

Much depends on your activities. Most people's basic needs can be met from fresh natural foods and water. But if you're working in heavy industry, in hot temperatures or with a lot of exertion, salt has to be replaced. Doctors used to recommend salt tablets for athletes or strenuous workers, but today they prefer that salt be taken in other than tablet form. Salt tablets can be dangerous and even contribute to dehydration by attracting water to the stomach, away from other cells in the body where water is needed. The most important concern is replacing lost fluid.

For young babies, the US Recommended Daily Dietary Allowance is 150mg of sodium, so salt is no longer included in American jars of baby food. Infants have been known to die from serious overdoses of salt, as their kidneys are not sufficiently developed to cope with excesses. A recent news item reported the death of an 11-month-old child in Boston, Massachusetts, after three dessertspoons of table salt had been inadvertently mixed into the baby formula in a hospital. But death can also occur from heat prostration and salt depletion in hot weather, and children can quickly become dehydrated from sweating and diarrhoea.

Elderly people can also be very sensitive to salt loss and should avoid the frequent use of diuretics that deplete the body of sodium and potassium.

How Much is Too Much?

The connection between high salt consumption and hypertension is clear in other countries as well as Britain; in northern provinces of Japan, for example, where salt is still the main preservative, the daily intake is as much as six teaspoons, and in some villages high blood-pressure affects 40 per cent of the inhabitants. Stroke is still the leading cause of death in Japan, where the diet consists mostly of pickled vegetables, fish, seaweed and soya sauce.

A recent study of college students by the University of Illinois found they were indulging in especially high amounts of sodium: male students were consuming up to 13,956mg, with an average of 3904mg, and female students were eating up to 9374mg with an average of 2628mg per day. Much of this sodium was in the form of salted snacks, fast-food and soft drinks. Excessive sodium is definitely linked to high blood-pressure, so the poor food habits of young people could lead to severe problems sooner or later.

On the other hand, there are areas of the world where primitive people eat little salt in their food, where hypertension is virtually unheard of and inhabitants do not suffer high blood-pressure with advancing years — for instance, tribesmen of rural Uganda, Brazilian Indians, Alaskan Eskimos, and people of the high country of Malaysia and New Guinea.

But blood-pressure can climb when salt is introduced into a salt-free culture: between 1966 and 1972, a study conducted by a Harvard team headed by Dr Lot Page, took a close look at six tribes in the Solomon Islands. Three of the tribes were entirely isolated from Western culture, and the other three (also 'primitive') got to eat heavily-salted tinned ham and beef jerky supplied to them by Chinese traders. Only in the second group did blood-pressure increase with age. And in the tribe that traditionally cooked its fish and vegetables in sea-water, blood-pressure was the highest. Dr. Page reported, 'When we analysed all the components of change, diet always showed up as the key factor.'

So the high intake of salt in the Western diet is thus largely unnecessary and definitely unhealthy, leading as it does to a plague of premature death and disease.

It would be true to say that, without some sodium compounds, many commercial products could not be made as we know them today, although companies are constantly discovering new formulas and *are* able to reduce the amounts of salt and sodium in processing.

But isn't it time to say 'enough' and reduce the sodium that goes into your body? While it's still not easy to say in advance just who will be sensitive to salt and susceptible to high blood-pressure, most doctors believe that, as a society, we would benefit by cutting down on sodium.

LET'S DO IT! BE A SALT-WATCHER!

2
What Can We Do About It?

Eating is one of life's pleasures, but you don't have to give up enjoyment of meals when you leave out salt and sodium. In fact, you'll gradually find that you are getting the true flavours of foods and not just the salt taste on the tip of your tongue.

Cardinal Rules for Salt-Watchers

1. Buy only fresh meats, fresh vegetables, fresh fruits.
2. Be a label reader of processed, tinned and frozen foods (see the list of 'E' numbers on page 29).
3. Look critically at your menus; revise recipes.
4. Put away your salt-cellar and other seasonings with salt.
5. Increase your use of herbs and spices; garnish dishes prettily, making the most use of colour.
6. Know what's in your water supply, other drinks, and medicines.

When You Shop

Cyril Connolly, the famous critic and author, once punned about the midday meal in South Africa consisting mainly of the 'cold table' which he said 'covers a multitude of tins'. And in Britain also we do indeed use many tinned goods and have come to rely on some canned staples. However, choosing fresh vegetables, meats, fish and poultry that have had little or no processing, results in the greatest sodium savings.

Be a label reader: When you *must* use processed, tinned or frozen products in your meals, read the labels critically for the list of ingredients, when you shop. Here are some danger signals:

Salt or salted	Brine or brined
Pickled	Cured
Smoked	Kippered
Soya sauce	Self-raising
Baking powder	Baking soda
Bicarbonate of soda	Na
Any ingredient with 'sodium' in its name, such as monosodium glutamate or disodium phosphate.	

Remember that 'low calorie' or 'dietetic' does *not* indicate reduced amounts of sodium. Use the sodium information tables at the back of this Guide to help you select low-sodium foods, and copy the list of 'E' numbers on page 29 onto a postcard to carry with you when shopping.

Some companies don't list ingredients fully on their product labels but will give nutrition information to customers who write for it, so look for the firm's address on the label.

An improvement in the labelling of the salt/sodium content of processed foods is desperately needed in the UK if we are to have a choice, so that those who prefer a low-sodium diet can select suitable foods. In the booklet entitled '*Look at the Label*' prepared for the Ministry of Agriculture, Fisheries and Food by the Central Office of Information in 1982, (H.M.S.O.), it is stated that 'Food labelling laws are there to inform you. . . . In these days of convenience foods, informative labels are more important than ever. . .'

Clear labelling that is easily understandable by everyone needs to be provided, giving the total salt content and the amount of sodium per serving. Ideally, foods would be categorized into salt groups — 'low', 'moderate' or 'high' so that shoppers could see at a glance the amount of sodium they are really getting for their money.

In the USA, clear nutritional labelling of products is mandatory, and the list of low-sodium food items gets longer all the time: food companies have introduced many unsalted lines that are being given more shelf-space in the mainstream of American supermarkets — not hidden in the 'dietetic' section at the back of the shop or sold only at the chemists.

In Finland, legislation limits the salt content of soups and gravy mixes to a maximum level of 1 per cent, and voluntary agreements were reached to reduce salt in bread, cheeses, etc. And in Belgium, where the people were formerly heavy salt users, legislation has been introduced to reduce the amount of salt added to bread, and encouragement is given to the production of salt-free foods and the clear labelling of the salt content in foods.

With the public becoming more aware of the quantities of sodium in processed food, and how damaging that sodium can be to their health, they will reject highly-salted items and demand that sodium be reduced or eliminated entirely. If we stop buying food with excessive salt, maybe the food manufacturers will stop selling it. We can create the demand for 'no-salt-added' foods.

Food companies may protest that reducing or eliminating salt cannot be done on a large scale without economic losses, as the average shopper expects to find the taste of salt in food and would consider saltless food too bland. However, many American food manufacturers are marketing 'reduced-sodium' food items with great success, alongside the customary salted varieties, proving that it does not mean commercial suicide, but an opportunity to expand markets and profits.

A few British food companies are distributing unsalted or low-sodium foods, and some are listed at the back of this Guide.

Look at the shelves in your neighbourhood grocer or supermarket, and tell the manager you want to see more unsalted foods. Write letters to the Consumers' Association and enlist their support in getting more unsalted foods on the market. Petition the big cereal companies to reduce the salt in breakfast foods. Why does your baker put large quantities of salt in your bread? It's mostly unnecessary and avoidable — tell him so. Why not return to unsalted potato crisps, with the salt in a small separate sachet to be added or not, according to *your* taste? Why put salt in yogurt when there is no technical reason for it? Why put huge amounts of salt in butter (as much as 3.5 grams per 100 grams)? Travellers to Europe know and enjoy the unsalted butter that is more popular there. With refrigeration being widespread today, the heavy use of salt in butter and margarine is unnecessary. Sodium nitrite is often essential to preserve meats and stop the growth of harmful bacteria, but it also gives a red colour to make meats more appealing to the eye; sodium in the form of polyphosphates is often added to poultry to make the birds hold in more water and appear juicy. The meat processors could therefore cut down on a proportion of the sodium compounds they use.

In cheeses, sodium chloride is used in the preparation to control texture and prevent the growth of unwanted bacteria but allowing the Lactobacilli to develop in different cheese varieties; most tins of vegetables are in brine, unnecessary for preservation; pickled and fermented vegetables have large amounts of salt. Food processors should make reductions in salt in these areas.

Revise Your Recipes

Consider the total amount of sodium in a meal, or in a day's meals, using the sodium tables in this Guide. If you eat a high-sodium food, choose a low-sodium food to go with it, or serve reduced-sodium food at your next meal. Take into consideration not only the sodium content of a food, but how much you will eat. Consider also the proportion or balance of calories and essential nutrients in the food.

When you start with basic recipes at home, you're in charge of the amount of salt you add. Reduce the salt you add to foods during cooking. They say the ability to taste salt may decline in our later years, so don't over-salt to compensate. Cut back gradually. Go through your cookery books: try gradually reducing the amounts of salt, baking powder and bicarbonate of soda in your favourite recipes until you've got them down to half or less — or none at all. In any case, if you cook with a microwave oven, salt should be avoided because it actually draws liquid out of food and interferes with the microwave cooking pattern. Consider the sodium content of all the ingredients in a recipe. For instance, if you use cured meat, dehydrated or tinned soup, cheese or tinned vegetables in a dish, you may not need to add any salt. Look for sauces and condiments with less sodium, or use lemon juice, spices or herbs — such as onion or garlic powder (*not* onion or garlic salt), paprika, pepper, curry or dill — for flavour. Make your own relishes, pickles and salad dressings — cutting back on the salt. Avoid bouillon or stock cubes, beef and vegetable extracts, meat tenderizers, soya sauce, Worcestershire and brown sauces, and ready-prepared mustards and horseradish.

Salt-Cellars

The biggest step in your 'Salt-Watching' strategy will be to reduce table salt, as well as the cooking-salt jar. Try some of the following ideas, and see which works best for you and your family:

1. Take a fresh look at your salt-cellars and quietly store away those with extra-large holes. Scientists have been experimenting with hole-sizes for shakers and they prefer a single hole. 1/10 inch (2.5mm) in diameter or less.
2. Try one shake of salt instead of two.
3. Make the holes slightly moist, so it's harder to shake the salt. Plug up some of the holes.
4. Put the salt-cellar on the table but keep it empty to help overcome the automatic habit.
5. Omit the salt-cellar from the table; you may forget you need it.
6. Fill the salt-cellar with your own blend of seasonings and herbs instead of salt. Recipes later in this chapter.

It's important to remember that sea salt and rock salt, although enjoying current popularity, are identical to ordinary table salt with perhaps additional trace elements. The minerals in sea salt are mostly removed when it is processed, to eliminate sand, fish-parts and dirt. Sea salt is just as hazardous as ordinary table salt, which incidentally was also salt from a sea at one time.

Salt Alternatives

The salt-processing companies and seasoning makers are producing substitutes for salt — usually more expensive than salt, and some brands are found only in pharmacies and health food shops. But these alternatives merely perpetuate your desire for salt-flavoured foods; far better to teach your taste-buds not to crave the salty taste. Before buying a substitute, read the label carefully to find the words 'sodium free' or 'low-sodium salt substitute', as some of them may still contain a high proportion of sodium — 'low salt' does not indicate 'no salt'. Generally the salt substitutes contain varying amounts of potassium chloride, calcium chloride or ammonium chloride, instead of sodium chloride, so check with your doctor before switching, because under some medical conditions (e.g., kidney problems) such alternatives can be dangerous.

Salt substitutes can taste bitter if included during cooking so they are generally added at the last minute, but gourmet cooks tend to avoid them entirely, preferring to use herbs and spices generously as more healthy alternative seasonings.

A word of caution to vegetarians and families living near the coast who may use dried *sea lettuce* or other seaweeds as alternatives in their salt-cellars: the sodium in seaweeds can be high and is not recommended for Salt-Watchers. In some parts of the country, *laver* or *laverbread* is valued for its mineral salt content as well as other nutrients, but it *is* high in sodium and *not* for Salt-Watchers; neither is *dulse* seaweed, for between-meal nibbling.

Herbs and Spices

Herbs and spices used with skill can easily substitute for salt and make an ordinary dish into a heavenly gourmet one. Interesting spices can add zing or be intriguing, and a squeeze of lemon juice or a little grated peel can bring a fresh tang to your meals. Experiment!

But first, let's have some definitions to help you become more familiar with the world of spices:

Spices: Aromatic natural products from tropical regions. Dried seeds, buds, fruits, flower parts, bark or roots of plants.
Herbs: Usually from temperate areas. Aromatic leaves, flowers of plants.
Seeds: Usually of temperate origin. They are aromatic, dried, small whole fruits or seeds.

As salt has a history related to many parts of the world, spices also have a romance dating back to the beginning of recorded time. The search for spices sent thousands of men to their deaths on dangerous caravan routes and uncharted oceans, caused raids and wars, and inspired men to journey into the unknown and discover lands that they hadn't dreamed existed. Spices were in use long before written records. Ancient Chinese writings tell of the spice trade in the year 200 BC, and a flourishing spice business early in the first century AD. Rome came into the spice trade during the last half of the first century, enjoying a lucrative business with China and what is now India, for spices, aromatic woods and fragrant oils.

These exotic goods were in extremely short supply and therefore expensive, having to be transported by camel over long tortuous routes from Southern India, through Afghanistan, Persia, Syria and Arabia to the ports on the Mediterranean. The spice caravans were often attacked by bandits and always at the mercy of the weather.

In the ninth century, cloves and mace sold for the equivalent of £12 a pound. Pepper was so costly, it was sold by the individual peppercorn! High prices attracted unscrupulous traders who made fortunes by adulterating the small quantities of spices they were able to obtain and selling them at astronomical prices. Adulteration of spices became so widespread that authorities in Rome, Baghdad and Alexandria decreed that it would be punishable by death. Large numbers of entrepreneurs actually did lose their heads over spices!

'For a bag of pepper they would cut each other's throats without hesitation'. (*Joseph Conrad*) For several hundred years the secrets of the Indies were known to only a few caravan masters, mostly Arabians, taking pains to keep secret the sources of their valuable cargoes, by spreading exaggerated and fantastic stories of monsters, dragons, fierce wild men and other dangers of the trails.

But during the last half of the thirteenth century, Marco Polo travelled extensively through the Near East, Asia and island chains of the Pacific and stumbled on the sources of the spice trade. He told glowing stories of seeing ginger growing in China, cinnamon in Ceylon, pepper in Borneo, and of nutmeg and clove trees growing on volcanic islands jutting out of the Indian and Pacific Oceans. Moreover, he had returned from his journey part-way by sea, thus proving there might be a sea passage to the Indies less perilous than the caravan routes. For the next two hundred years many brave navigators sailed into the unknown, especially the Portuguese with their armoured galleons and speedy caravels, seeking a practical route to the wealth of spices growing in the East, pushing back the boundaries of the known world and opening whole new continents to exploration. The Magellan round-the-world expedition of 1519-23 finally charted a course to the islands of the East Indies, returning to Spain with news that was to have a profound impact on the spice trade.

Spices and herbs should still be treasured.

Check spices for freshness, buy only the top brands, write the date of purchase on the labels and check your supply frequently so that the flavours are at their peak with a full aroma and bright colour. Whole spices generally keep longer than ground spices. Store them carefully in a cool, dry place, keeping containers tightly closed after each use to retain the flavour and prolong the life of the spice. Be sure to keep them away from the heat of the kitchen stove, the damp of the sink and out of direct sunlight. If you buy them in cardboard containers, transfer to airtight screwtop jars or small metal tins.

Spices vary tremendously, depending upon their country of origin, and how carefully they are processed, ground and packaged. Measure herbs first, then crush between your fingers to release the greatest flavours. When experimenting with what might be a new herb to you, be cautious: crush a little in your hand and let it warm before sniffing and testing. If it seems delicate, you can probably use it boldly. If it's very pungent, be cautious and try only a little at first. Generally ¼ teaspoon of a dried herb or spice is enough for four servings, with the exception of curry and chilli powder that usually add a more robust pungency.

If herbs are used in an uncooked recipe, such as a salad dressing, prepare well before the meal, and add herbs several hours before serving. Refrigerate 3 to 4 hours or overnight. For soups and stews that take long cooking, add herbs during the last hour of cooking. For baked or roasted foods, sprinkle on the herbs just before cooking, or make a herb-butter to top portions at serving-time.

Start growing your own herbs in the garden or window-box. Parsley and mint are easy to grow. Adding fresh herbs to salads greatly enhances the flavours of crisp greens. Discard stems as they may be bitter, then snip the leaves small with kitchen scissors or chop finely on a board.

To dry your own herbs for storage during the winter, wash them and remove parts you don't wish to preserve. Spread on a tray and dry in an oven no warmer than 90° to 100°F (32° to 38°C), until the leaves feel crackly dry, between 24 and 48 hours. Alternatively you can tie bunches of herbs together (2 or 3 stems) with string; hang upside down in the kitchen, garage or garden shed until dry, which will take about two weeks. Herbs can also be dried between paper towels in the microwave, on a low setting. Watch closely so they don't char.

Fresh herbs can also be frozen. Wash herbs and pat dry between paper towels. Remove and discard the stems of basil, mint, oregano, parsley and sage. Spread herbs on a tray or baking sheet and freeze. When frozen, transfer to plastic containers with tight-fitting lids. Be sure to label the containers and date them. After a short time flavours may change due to the high amount of volatile oils in these flavourful plants.

Generally, 1 dessertspoon of fresh herbs equals 1 teaspoon of dried herbs, but flavours are variable, and it's better to err on the side of too little rather than too much, and add more later if necessary, according to your family's tastes.

Experiment with making your own herb-vinegars for salads. Cider vinegar has many uses for the Salt-Watcher in salads, soups and gravies. Commercial herb vinegars and wine vinegars may tend to contain a little more sodium.

Look at the Chart on page 113 and you can see that herbs and spices have a negligible amount of sodium in them, so can be used freely by Salt-Watchers. Many herbs and spices may complement the flavour of a dish, but don't try combining too many at one time. The best combinations with foods are those that taste right for you and your family. Express yourself! You don't have to go by the book.

For your own blend of seasonings in the salt-cellar, try these combinations:

Garden Blend

1 dessertspoon garlic powder
1½ teaspoons onion powder
1 teaspoon ground basil
1 teaspoon ground parsley
1½ teaspoons ground black pepper
1 teaspoon dried sage
½ teaspoon nutmeg
Dash of cayenne pepper

Grandma's Herbs

2 teaspoons dry mustard
1 teaspoon dried thyme
1 teaspoon ground black pepper
2 teaspoons paprika
4 teaspoons onion powder
2 teaspoons garlic powder

And consider some of these great go-togethers:

With asparagus	lemon juice, white pepper, nutmeg.
With broccoli	lemon juice, mustard, paprika.
With cabbage	nutmeg, onion, black pepper, vinegar, celery seeds, fennel.

What Can We Do About It?

With cauliflower	lemon juice, black pepper, celery seeds.
With corn	fresh tomato, pimento, green pepper.
With courgettes	onion, tomato, pimento, garlic, basil, oregano.
With cucumbers	vinegar, dill, chives, spring onions.
With mushrooms	nutmeg, pepper, paprika.
With fresh peas	fresh mint, parsley, onions, fresh mushrooms, dash of sugar, dill.
With potatoes	fresh black pepper, chopped green pepper, onions, chives, fresh mint, parsley, mace, nutmeg.
With red cabbage	vinegar and sugar, onion, apple, nutmeg, cloves, pepper.
With rice	fresh mushrooms, onion, tomato, pimento, chives, saffron, curry powder, chilli powder.
With tomatoes	oregano, onion, chives, basil, marjoram.

Some other *seasoning* ideas:
- Try Five-Spice powder, usually found in Oriental markets. This is a blend of ground cloves, ginger, cinnamon, nutmeg and anise, so if it's not available in your neighbourhood, you can concoct your own mix.
- Add a dash of hot-pepper sauce, Worcestershire sauce or soya sauce to recipes — they *do* contain sodium but much less than salt.
- Consider dashes of sherry or rum to add an exciting difference to fruit cups and fruit pies.
- Lemons can substitute for salt in many ways: adding zest to soups and gravies, sparking up salad dressings instead of or as well as vinegar, blended into marinades and your own barbecue sauce, enlivening fish dishes, making vegetables more appealing to your family, and giving a tang to desserts.

Extra *garnishes* will make the whole family enjoy your salt-free meals: try for pretty colour combinations of foods — the bright red of tomatoes, the rich yellow of fresh corn — together with some of the following ideas:

- Radish roses, or rows of thinly sliced radishes.
- Generous sprigs of parsley, watercress or mint leaves.
- Cucumber slices with dainty edges made with the tines of a fork.
- Thinly sliced mushrooms, dipped in lemon juice to preserve colour.
- Avocado pears sliced in different ways, also with a dip of lemon juice.
- Green or red pepper strips.
- Finely chopped chives.
- Hard-boiled egg slices or wedges.
- Lemons cut in simple wedges, thin slices, cartwheels or roses.
- Lemons made into small cups with serrated edges, to hold individual servings of dips, dressings and lemon butter.

3
An A-to-Z Guide to Cutting Salt and Sodium

APPLES, PEARS, PLUMS, BANANAS, PEACHES:
  These fresh fruits are great for Salt-Watchers, raw or baked. Tinned fruit may have sodium if it was used to remove skins, or if ascorbic acid (sodium ascorbate) was added to enhance flavour. Tinned apple sauce is all right but not the ready-prepared dry mix. Avoid dried sulphured apples.

BACON AND GAMMON:
  High-sodium and absolutely taboo for Salt-Watchers!

BAKED BEANS:
  Avoid tinned baked beans, tinned spaghetti in tomato sauce, and other commercial toppings for toast. For quick snacks on toast, grill a few tomatoes or mushrooms, dusted with herbs or Parmesan. Beans are highly nutritious, but should be prepared from dry measures, cooked without salt or bicarbonate of soda.

BAKING POWDER:
  Reduce the quantity of powder in recipes. If your doctor approves the use of potassium, make your own sodium-free baking powder:

Sodium-Free Baking Powder

2 tablespoons cream of tartar (potassium bitartrate)
2 tablespoons arrowroot starch
2 tablespoons potassium bicarbonate

Salfree low-sodium brand is available in some stores. Low-sodium baking powders generally need 1½ times the amount of standard baking powders in recipes.

BAKING SODA:
See under Bicarbonate of Soda.
BEEF:
Avoid corned beef and dried chipped beef, commercial beefburgers, pies and sausages.
BEEF AND VEGETABLE EXTRACTS:
To be shunned. The makers should be encouraged to bring out low-sodium varieties.
BERRIES:
Blackberries, raspberries, gooseberries, strawberries, cherries, are all fine, especially the fresh fruit rather than tinned.
BICARBONATE OF SODA:
To be avoided. When making scones, adapt your favourite recipe by adding an extra egg-white to the mixture. Have eggs at room temperature before beating thoroughly and stirring into the dough. Potassium bicarbonate is available at chemists as a low-sodium baking soda, if your doctor approves the use of potassium.
BISCUITS, CRACKERS AND CRISPBREADS:
Even sweet biscuits are salted and include much sodium (baking powder or bicarbonate of soda), and commercial bakeries include many other sodium compounds to improve texture, flavour, etc. Low-sodium sweet biscuits are at some chemists (*Rite-Diet* for example). Make your own biscuits and oatcakes, eliminating salt, reducing baking powder quantities and using plain flour. Crackers for cheese and crispbreads often have salt sprinkled on top as well as salt and sodium inside; look for unsalted biscuits and matzohs, or unsalted *Ryvita*. Or you can make your own crackers.
BREADS AND ROLLS:
Most commercial breads have a high proportion of salt which could be reduced by the large and small bakers if the public demanded it. *Rite-Diet* low-sodium bread is available at chemists, or you can make yeast bread at home with no salt, revising the times for rising and kneading, as the rising time of 'saltless' dough may be shorter. Never use self-raising flour. Ready-made sweet rolls or buns using yeast are preferable to those made with baking powder or bicarbonate of soda.

BREAKFAST CEREALS:

Many of the dry cereals are relatively high in sodium, especially bran cereals. Refer to the sodium tables in the Appendix. *Shredded Wheat* and *Puffed Wheat* are lower in sodium content. If you need fibre, sprinkle on natural *unprocessed* wheat bran or wheat germ. Make your own muesli in preference to the ready-made. Hot cooked cereals, including porridge, *Ready Brek* and *Warm Start*, prepared in unsalted water, are preferred for a low-sodium regimen. Top cereals with sliced bananas, strawberries or chopped apple; instead of sugar, stir in a drop or two of vanilla essence or a sprinkle of cinnamon to give a suggestion of sweetness.

CAKES:

Bakers' cakes and the ready-boxed dry mixes for cakes, scones and biscuits are generally high-sodium, with sodium compounds used for texturing, flavouring and prolonging shelf-life. When you make your own cakes at home, *you* can control the sodium by eliminating the salt, reducing baking powder, or using low-sodium baking powder, and plain flour. Avoid self-raising flour. If more leavening is needed, an extra egg-white will help. Eggs should be at room temperature before beating thoroughly and folding in.

CHEESES:

Be choosy about your cheeses! Avoid Stilton, Roquefort, Danish Blue, Gorgonzola and similar blue-veined cheeses; shun processed cheeses and cheese-spreads, Camembert and Féta. Select a mild Cheddar, a simple unprocessed Emmenthal (Swiss) cheese or cream cheese. Cottage cheeses can vary; some have added salt during the processing. Although Parmesan is high-sodium, a light sprinkle on unsalted vegetables can give them a lift. Never use salt in recipes that use cheese.

CHICKEN:

Roast chicken (meat only)	81mg
Chicken pie (frozen)	1926mg

Let these sodium figures speak for themselves. Avoid convenience and take-away foods; avoid ready-boxed seasoned coatings and stuffing mixes, and commercial dry mixes for sauces.

Chicken can be 'oven fried' using no fat: toss chicken pieces in beaten egg, then in your own blend of breadcrumbs, wheat germ, bran or plain flour, plus herbs, etc. for a healthy crunchy crust. Bake in a shallow pan in a hot oven for about an hour. When roasting chicken (or turkey), baste with a mixture of unsalted butter or margarine, paprika and lemon juice. Make your own stuffing with breadcrumbs, plenty of chopped onion, and a variety of herbs. Or simply stuff with a whole skinned onion, a small piece of celery stalk and a small carrot.

CITRUS:
Grapefruit, oranges, lemons, tangerines are fine. Use plenty, to give zesty flavouring and colourful garnishing.

COCOA AND CHOCOLATE:
Cocoa powder and chocolate drinking compounds are high-sodium. When using chocolate in recipes, select plain bars to grate or melt into the mixture, or unsweetened baking chocolate.

COFFEE AND TEA:
Standard infused tea or coffee, or instant coffee, is permissible, depending on your water supply (see Chapter 5). Avoid the instant coffee powders that have special flavourings and concentrated essences.

CONDIMENTS AND SAUCES:
Avoid brown sauce, tomato sauce, sweet pickles, chutneys, piccalilli, Worcestershire, soya sauce, and ready-prepared mustards. Mix mustard from the dry powder. Make your own chutney or pickles. Shun the dry mixes for making onion sauce, parsley sauce, sweet and sour sauce, and the tinned or bottled cooking sauces, commercial mint jellies and ready-made mint sauces.

DESSERTS AND PUDDINGS:
Ready-made powders for puddings and custards, and puddings in tins, are high-sodium. Choose fresh or stewed fruit for a low-sodium diet, home-made jellies and home-made blancmange. When making sweets at home, the results are not affected by omitting the salt. Use unsalted margarine and plain flour. Splash fruit cups or compotes with a squeeze of lemon juice or a little sherry, rum or brandy for a special treat.

DRIED FRUITS:
Although fresh fruits are generally low in sodium, dried apricots, figs, sultanas, raisins and currants often have sodium added during their processing and packaging. Reduce amounts of dried fruits in recipes, and 'extend' by chopping finely before adding to mixtures.

EGGS:
When hard-boiling eggs for salads or devilling, drop a few onion slices or onion flakes into the boiling water. The eggs will be delicately flavoured and there'll be no need for salt. Sauté finely-chopped onions or green pepper in unsalted margarine before scrambling eggs. Add plenty of cracked black pepper. Or dust with Parmesan cheese and a shake of paprika. When adding eggs to home-made low-sodium cake recipes, bring the eggs to room temperature first and beat thoroughly before adding to the mixture, as the lightness will depend on them.

FATS:
Shop for unsalted margarine with only about 1 to 2mg sodium per tablespoon. Unsalted low-fat spreads are becoming available. Vegetable oils are sodium-free; lard and suet are generally low-sodium.

FISH:
Avoid commercial fish cakes and fish fingers. Fin-fish are generally lower-sodium than shellfish, and freshwater fish are lower than ocean-caught fish. Packs of frozen fish may be processed with salt. Read the labels. Avoid smoked herrings, kippers, salt-cod, tinned salmon, tunafish, shrimp and crab. If you must use these tinned items in recipes, drain off the liquid and rinse with clear tap water for a few minutes. This can reduce the sodium by as much as 75 per cent. Fresh fish, grilled or baked, can have a zest with plenty of lemon juice, with wedges on the side, or experiment with countless combinations of herbs in white sauce — curry, marjoram, paprika, bay leaf. Garnish colourfully.

FRANKFURTERS, SAUSAGES:
Frankfurters, beef and pork sausages, hot dogs, are all high-sodium and to be eschewed if you want to lower your sodium intake.

FRUIT JUICES:
When shopping for fruit juice, be sure you're buying pure juice and not a blend or concocted drink with added sodium to sharpen flavour. Buy orange, grapefruit or pineapple juice, but avoid tomato juice, tomato juice cocktail or vegetable juice cocktail since these are usually seasoned with salt. Shun powders that mix to make into juice drinks.

GELATINE:
Ignore the ready-made dessert jellies, but make desserts with fresh fruit juices and plain setting agent: almost as quick, but far more wholesome, without the sodium additives frequently added for flavouring.

GRAVY MIXES AND STOCK CUBES:
To be avoided until the food manufacturers can bring out low-sodium varieties. Make your own simple sauces and gravies, using plenty of herbs in a brown or white sauce.

GREEN VEGETABLES:
If you need to clean dirt and insects from cabbage, sprouts, etc., rinse with vinegar and not salt in the washing water. Cook all vegetables in unsalted water, and no baking soda. Dress up greens with a dash of vinegar, onion, pepper or nutmeg. If you like garlic, add two or more halved garlic cloves when cooking, but discard when serving.

HAM:
With such a high-sodium content, ham is best completely avoided, along with bacon and gammon. If you have to have it for a meal, rinse the joint in several changes of fresh tap water and boil the piece rather than baking, grilling or frying.

JAMS, JELLIES AND SWEET SPREADS:
Golden syrup, black treacle and commercially made lemon curd have large amounts of sodium. Shop for marmalade, pure honey or fruit jams. Jams labelled 'low calorie' may contain sodium saccharin, or ascorbic acid and are best avoided by Salt-Watchers. Making jams and jellies at home is the best way to avoid sodium, using the freshest fruits in season.

LAMB:
Lamb chops may be sprinkled with Italian-type seasoning (basil,

sage, rosemary, marjoram and thyme) plus lemon juice. Who needs salt? Many other spices enhance roast lamb: ginger, caraway seed, garlic powder. Or try thin slivers of garlic or lemon strips inserted in slits before roasting. Season lamb gravy with red wine, or a trace of instant coffee.

MAYONNAISE:

Mayonnaise is fairly high in sodium, but French dressing is even higher. Thin with lemon juice or vinegar to reduce the proportion of sodium. 'Low calorie' commercial mayonnaise still has a significant amount of sodium. Make your own mayonnaise, fresh and wholesome and low-sodium; better still, dress salads with simple oil and vinegar.

MEAT AND FISH PASTES AND PÂTÉS:

To circumvent the high-sodium in these products, make your own pastes and pâtés, using leftover cooked meats and fish moistened with a little home-made mayonnaise or unsalted margarine, seasoned with herbs.

NUTS:

Straight from the shell, they are generally low-sodium. Obvious taboos are the salted nut snacks, salted peanut butters and pickled walnuts.

ONIONS, GARLIC AND CHIVES:

The onion and garlic families of vegetables are low-sodium; use plenty of these to make dishes and sauces more flavoursome. Avoid pickled onions.

PANCAKES, CRÊPES:

Ready-boxed pancake mix and commercial preparations for crêpes are high-sodium. Make your own from simple ingredients. Spark up pancakes with powdered or crystallized ginger, or cinnamon. Or add grated raw apple.

PANCAKE SYRUP, GOLDEN SYRUP AND TREACLE:

These products are high in sodium compounds. Use pure honey or pure maple syrup.

PEANUT BUTTERS:

They generally have added salt, so read the labels carefully. Some health food shops may have unsalted nut butters derived from nuts that have been freshly ground.

PEAS, GREEN BEANS, CORN AND OTHER VEGETABLES:
Use fresh vegetables whenever possible. A tablespoon of tinned peas can contain as much sodium as 5½ pounds of fresh ones! Some frozen vegetables have been processed with sodium during sorting, so check the label or write to the food company. Canned vegetables, especially peas, are usually high-sodium unless otherwise labelled; peas are sorted in brine during canning. The canning liquid should be drained off and the vegetables rinsed in a colander under running water to reduce sodium. Lightly cook all vegetables in unsalted water, even though most directions specify salt. *Del Monte* has recently launched a line of low-sodium tinned vegetables that will be in some shops.

PICKLES, PICCALILLI, SAUCES AND CHUTNEYS:
Try substituting sliced cucumbers or courgettes, marinated in mild vinegar for a few hours.

PIES:
Eschew commercial beef or pork pies, sausage rolls, pasties and sweet pies, and ready-made pie-crusts. Make your own pies at home, omitting salt from pastry and filling, using plain flour, low-sodium baking powder or reducing the quantity of ordinary baking powder.

PORK:
Fresh roast pork is acceptable, but not pork that has been salted, cured or pickled.

POTATOES:
A simple potato is low-sodium, but once it gets into a tin, or processed into instant powder or made into crisps it can pick up a lot of sodium along the way.

Example (per 100g):

New potato, boiled	41mg sodium
New potato, canned	260mg sodium
Instant powder, reconstituted	260mg sodium
Potato crisps	550mg sodium

Cook fresh potatoes in unsalted water (add a sprig of mint leaf, maybe, or several slices of onion); mash with unsalted margarine, and plenty of freshly-ground black pepper, chopped chives, spring onions, parsley or nutmeg. Season home fried potatoes with basil or sage instead of salt, and with a shake of vinegar.

SALADS:

Have the freshest crispiest greens, best quality tomatoes, green peppers, chopped spring onions, and experiment with sprinklings of herbs. Commercial salad creams and salad dressings are high-sodium. Dilute with vinegar or lemon juice. Make your own mayonnaise. Or make your own simple dressing from oil, vinegar, a big dash of lemon juice and cracked pepper. Avoid commercially canned coleslaw, vegetable and potato salads.

SAUCES AND PICKLES:

See Condiments and Sauces.

SNACKS:

Obviously taboo for Salt-Watchers are salted potato crisps, salted popcorn, pretzel sticks, salted nuts and black and green olives. Prepare fresh relish trays of raw vegetables that have plenty of crunch: celery sticks, carrot sticks, cucumber strips, courgette strips, pepper strips, cauliflowerets and crisp radishes.

SOUPS:

Condensed, ready-to-serve, instant and dehydrated soups are very high-sodium. Make your own soups, broths and stockpots using natural ingredients and your own blends of herbs and spices. Try to make soups and stews the day before you need them, so you can skim off any accumulated fat. Make soups with more vegetables than meat, to fill you up without adding calories. Divide the soup or stew into individual portions and store in the freezer.

SPAGHETTI, MACARONI, NOODLES, RICE AND BARLEY:

Avoid tinned spaghetti and other pastas in high-sodium sauces. Avoid meat-flavoured rice mixes. Cook raw wholemeal spaghetti and brown rice in unsalted water with a teaspoon of salad oil or unsalted butter or margarine. Most seasonings can be derived from the accompanying sauces, but you can season pasta with lemon juice. When making your own pasta sauce, use unsalted tomato purée or fresh chopped tomatoes in your favourite recipe. Spark up the flavour with a generous seasoning of herbs: bay leaf, oregano, garlic and lemon juice.

SWEETS AND CHOCOLATE:
If you're trying to lose a few pounds, sweets should be excluded. However if you have a sweet tooth, avoid toffees with their high-sodium content. Plain chocolate bars, fruit gums, jelly beans and some boiled sweets are generally lower in sodium.

TOMATOES:
Use fresh tomatoes whenever possible, as canned peeled tomatoes are often prepared with sodium to remove skins. Tomato sauce is high-sodium. Tomato purée can be thinned with water to substitute in recipes calling for tomato cooking sauce. Avoid tinned tomato juice and tomato juice cocktail.

TURKEY:
Shun self-basting turkeys: choose only fresh birds. The self-basting kind are often injected with a solution containing sodium phosphates to hold water in while the bird cooks. With a fresh, natural bird, baste it with the natural juices that flow, plus unsalted margarine with various herb combinations. Use no commercial stuffing mixes or dressings; make your own. Avoid ready-made turkey steaks.

ZUCCHINI/COURGETTES:
Prepare and cook according to guidelines for peas, green beans etc.

4
Where Are You Going?

Although you can carefully add up sodium and restrict it at home, the Salt-Watcher has to be cautious when eating out. Fast-food outlets, canteens, restaurants, delicatessens and cross-country travel all present their hazards when you want to reduce salt in your meals. But you can have a sensible strategy: if you have no alternative to high-sodium fast-foods for lunch, counterbalance with low-sodium foods for the breakfast and dinner you have at home. If a main dish is highly salted, balance it with no-salt accompanying dishes. If you have meals out frequently, keep in your pocket or handbag a personal salt-cellar containing your own blend of herbs and spices for discreet use.

Convenience and Fast-Foods

Let's look at some of the sodium levels in convenience foods:

Commercial beefburger (100g)	880mg sodium
Individual pork pie (100g)	720mg sodium
Individual steak and kidney pie (100g)	510mg sodium
Grilled pork sausage (85g)	1000mg sodium
Ham sandwich (white bread, 15g salted butter, 50g ham)	1025mg sodium

If you're having fish and chips for supper from your neighbourhood shop, ask them not to put salt on your order before it's handed to you; a good shake of malt vinegar is fine. Remove the batter coating, to eliminate the salty seasonings or baking powders that may have been added before the order was fried. By not eating the greasy coatings, you are also reducing the extra calories and cholesterol in the frying oil. Salads can be reliable fare, providing you order them with no ham or luncheon meat, or a bacon topping. Ask for your salads without salad cream or dressing, but have oil and vinegar on the side, so you can use your own discretion. When going out for a pizza, choose a simple style without the salty toppings of olives, anchovies, pepperoni and sausage that are taboo for Salt-Watchers.

Canteens and Restaurants

Get to be a regular at a few local restaurants so you can be familiar with their menus, and the staff can be aware of your special low-salt needs. If a dish on the menu is unknown to you, ask the waiter or waitress how it is prepared — don't guess! In the works canteen where you usually have a meal, have a chat with the cook, show her this book and discuss cutting down the amount of salt she uses, or have a word with the manager of your firm to pass the message along to the kitchen.

Instead of soups, which are often heavily salted, go for fresh fruit juices (not tomato juice), or fresh grapefruit halves (preferably not the tinned grapefruit segments), or a wedge of cantaloup for starters. Ask for unsalted margarine or low-fat spread with your roll. Order simple dishes, and ask that sauces or gravy be served on the side. If a dish is pre-cooked in a sauce, quietly spoon it off to the side of your plate, and check a little for saltiness.

If you are breakfasting away from home, instead of ham, sausages or bacon, ask for extra eggs (if your cholesterol count is not being monitored by your doctor), or order fresh fruit juices and low-sodium cereals such as *Shredded Wheat* or *Puffed Wheat*.

In ethnic restaurants (Oriental, for example), specify no MSG, soya sauce, garlic salt or onion salt in the dishes you order. Ask for vegetables to be prepared without salt; they should be fresh or frozen, but if you suspect they are canned, avoid them. Especially peas!

For pudding- and sweet-lovers, try to avoid gooey cakes, cream pies and brightly-coloured jellies. Choose fresh fruit in season, fruit salads, strawberries or grapes, and resist that topping of whipped cream.

If you don't have a sweet tooth, but prefer to see the cheeseboard, be careful in your selection: cream cheese, a simple Cheddar, an unprocessed Swiss — avoiding the blue-veined types, Camembert, Féta, and processed cheeses wrapped in silver-paper. Ask for unseasoned crispbread, matzohs or Melba toast, since many biscuits-for-cheese have salted coatings.

Many more diners are requesting no-salt dishes as more people are becoming health-conscious, so don't feel you're making a fuss! It's an expression of your good taste and your good judgment, and you can learn to assert yourself in a pleasant way in getting what you want. If the chef won't co-operate, you can take your patronage to an establishment where he will!

Delicatessen

If there's a delicatessen in your neighbourhood, be cautious if you're a Salt-Watcher, as these shops can be real minefields of high-sodium items like cold-cuts, sausages, imported cheeses, relishes and pickles. A cup of sauerkraut has about 1500mg of sodium; five large black Greek olives have over 400mg. Avoid the big gherkins, pickled beets, pickled walnuts and pickled onions and ready-prepared bean- or potato-salads. Choose simple ingredients such as Swiss cheese for sandwich fillings. If you eat meat, enquire if the turkey or chicken is freshly-cooked, as turkey rolls and other pre-cooked pressed meats can be high-sodium. Choose salads carefully, such as sliced cucumbers or carrot-and-raisin, or coleslaw, so long as it's not drenched with salad cream.

Meals with Friends

If you are to be a guest in a friend's home for a meal or for a longer stay, mention your preference for low-salt food to your host or hostess at the first opportunity, to avoid later embarrassment if you find salted food unpalatable.

The 'Jet Set'

For jet travellers or those on trains or cruise ships, specify low-sodium meals when booking holidays with your travel agent; and reconfirm your diet meal order when you check in. In hotel rooms you may be fortunate enough to have a small refrigerator so you can stock your own salt-free foods and snacks. It pays to ask for what you want when travelling. And if time allows, check the local water supply for sodium content when you arrive. If you go to a district where the water is high-sodium, bottled distilled water should be purchased for drinking.

Sandwich Lunches and Picnics

When you take a lunch-box every day, or go picnicking, you can exercise control over how much sodium you're having. Try to buy low-sodium bread — or bake your own with reduced salt. Make open-faced sandwiches. Or, as a change from bread, take Jewish matzohs, chapatis or unseasoned crispbreads or wafers. Try different filling combinations, like:

1. Well-rinsed tinned tunafish mixed with chopped celery and chopped apple, moistened with home-made mayonnaise.
2. Fish-salad (from previously grilled fish), home-made mayonnaise, dill-weed and freshly-ground black pepper.
3. Slice of unprocessed Swiss cheese, moistened with your own 'sandwich spread' of home-made mayonnaise, minced mild onion, shredded carrot and courgette, chopped celery and green pepper, with a dash of dill-weed, or tarragon, savory or basil.
4. Hard-boiled egg, finely chopped, mixed with chopped celery and green pepper, moistened with home-made mayonnaise.
5. Hard-boiled egg moistened with plain yogurt, with shredded carrots or courgettes, tarragon, chopped walnuts, and lettuce.
6. Spinach leaves (fresh and raw), hard-boiled egg, ¼ teaspoon minced mild onion (or pinch of onion powder), few drops of lemon juice, and home-made mayonnaise.
7. Cream cheese, hard-boiled egg slices and watercress sprigs.

8. Cream cheese, sprinkled with lemon juice and peel, and asparagus spears (cooked and chilled).
9. Cream cheese, thinned with a little pineapple juice, with banana slices and a sprinkle of flaked coconut.
10. And how about a Strawberry Cheesecake Sandwich with cream cheese, a few drops of lemon juice, fresh sliced strawberries and a dash of cinnamon?

Or, avoid bread altogether, and pack these into small plastic containers:
Hard-boiled eggs, plain or devilled.
Yogurt, plain or with fresh fruit.
Unsalted peanut butter stuffed into celery sticks or cucumber boats.

A wide-mouthed thermos can contain these:
Home-made stew or soups.
Home-made macaroni cheese.
Home-made baked beans.
A vegetable vinaigrette.
Fresh fruit, or baked apple, pear or peach.

Add raw vegetables to your lunch-box or picnic basket, wrapped separately in cellophane: carrot and celery sticks, radishes, green pepper strips, cauliflowerets, courgette strips, cucumber and tomato slices or wedges, and fresh watercress.

And fresh fruits in season: as a change from apples, oranges and bananas, try plums, pears, apricots, and cherries or grapes in small plastic bags.

5
What Are You Drinking?

Water

Scientists tells us that each cubic mile of sea water has 166 metric tons of salt. Traces of almost all the naturally occurring elements are found in sea-water, but more than three-quarters of the salt in the oceans is sodium chloride — that is, table salt. And the salinity of the oceans hasn't changed significantly for millions of years.

But the amount of sodium in fresh water supplies can vary enormously, and we ourselves have been changing the sodium levels in many parts of the world. When the sodium content of the soil is high, the sodium concentration in the ground water is also usually high, resulting in greater salinity of rivers, lakes and streams. As much as 50 per cent of the salt used on highways in winter to control ice and snow conditions goes into ground water. Water can also be affected by the run-off from sewage, industry and agriculture; near the coast there can be sea-water intrusion. Tap water can have sodium hypochlorite introduced as a disinfectant, and sodium fluoride added for controlling tooth decay. Under certain conditions, there can be higher readings of sodium in summer than in the winter months, or vice versa, depending on the amount of rainfall. So how much salt are you drinking?

Food is generally our major source of sodium, but where high sodium concentrations in the drinking water do occur, the contribution of sodium by water may amount to a significant percentage of your total sodium intake.

According to public health authorities, if your diet is restricted to 500mg to 1000mg of sodium per day, on doctor's orders, and you're drinking about 2 litres of water (8 glasses), the sodium level in your drinking water shouldn't be more than 20mg per litre. But of course, few people are on such a severe restriction of sodium by their physicians.

Nevertheless, if you are serious about knowing your total sodium intake each day, contact your local water board or filtration station to ascertain exactly what is coming out of your tap. Of course our water supplies are constantly and carefully supervised, monitored and filtered to safeguard purity, but if you have relatively high sodium levels in your community, you may consider it preferable to buy distilled or de-ionized bottled water for drinking and cooking. In any case, avoid drinking 'softened' water, as a home water-softener using a salt-system (not reverse-osmosis demineralization) will add up to 300mg of sodium per litre.

Imported and Domestic Bottled Mineral Waters

Many people prefer to drink bottled mineral water for their health, but may be adding a significant amount of sodium to their diet. Not all bottled water is 'mineral'. 'Mineral' means that the water once gushed directly from springs or has had minerals added later. Other containers of bottled water may have only water that has been purified by filtration or by chemicals. There are two varieties: still and effervescent. Sometimes the bubbles in mineral waters are Nature's own, when the label will say 'naturally sparkling', 'naturally carbonated' or 'naturally effervescent'; otherwise you can assume the bubbles have been created by the addition of carbon dioxide. Some bottled sparkling water is merely processed tap water: original minerals removed, a special combination of minerals added back to give the water a particular character, and then carbonated. Sparkling mineral waters, on the other hand, get their variety of delicate shadings not from the added minerals but their natural pH rating. Soft waters may show little character; very hard waters can taste 'soapy' or medicinal, somewhat like bicarbonate of soda.

Here's a partial list of some of the available brands:

Brand	Mg sodium per 8oz (240ml) glass	Comments
Apollinaris	127.1	very high
Badoit	2.05	almost sodium free
Bru	N/A	moderate
Caddo Valley	N/A	low
Calistoga	128	very high
Contrexeville	9	moderate
Evian	5.5	low
Fachingen	146.28	very high
Ferranelle	10.69	moderate
Fiuggi	6.8	low
Gerolsteiner Sprudel	30.8	moderate
Hisar	N/A	moderate
Mattoni	N/A	high
Perrier	2.8	almost sodium free
Poland Spring	.66	almost sodium free
Ramlosa	79	high
Saint Léger	N/A	moderate
Saint Yorre	N/A	very high
San Pellegrino	9.29	moderate
Sant Elena	28.1	moderate
Saratoga	16	moderate
Schweppes	12	moderate
Spa Reine	2.3	almost sodium free
Vichy Etat Célestin	.625	almost sodium free
Vitelloise	3	low
Volvic	8	moderate
Walzhauser	25	moderate

(Sodium figures courtesy of the International Bottled Water Association, Alexandria, VA, USA.)

Carbonated Beverages and Soft Drinks

The amount of sodium in soft drinks depends largely on the geographical location where the bottling is done and the local water supplies.

How many soft drinks do you have each day? The sodium can add up, especially with low-calorie diet beverages containing sodium saccharin, sodium benzoate and sodium chloride. 'Low-calorie' does *not* mean low-sodium, until the soft drink firms start producing drinks with reduced sodium, as they have in the United States.

Tonic water is generally low-sodium, but soda water is higher. Make your own soda with a syphon and carbon dioxide bulbs.

Pure lemon juice, squeezed from the fruit, has only 2mg of sodium per 100 millilitres (about 4 fl oz); but when the juice is made into lemon squash, the sodium content is multiplied ten times or more. (*Schweppes* lemon squash, undiluted, contains as much as 90mg sodium per 100 millilitres.)

Avoid crystals or powders to make fruit drinks; select pure juice, fresh, canned or frozen concentrate (but no tomato juice or tomato juice cocktail).

Make your own lemonade with pure fresh lemon juice, squeezed from the fruit (not from a plastic container), mixing juice and water in a jug or glass, sweetening to taste with a minimum of sugar. Another method of making lemonade is to scrub the skins of whole lemons, slice the fruit very thinly into a large bowl, pour boiling water over the fruit and allow to steep. Strain off the peel. Sweeten the lemonade to taste. This is best made early in the morning and allowed to cool.

Coffee, Tea, Cocoa, Milk

Fortunately we can still enjoy a good cup of percolated coffee, or tea, as there is only a trace of sodium, but avoid adding much milk as dairy products are relatively high in sodium content. When made from concentrated essence or from instant powder, coffee will contain larger amounts of sodium compounds due to the processing of the beans.

'Drink a pinta milka day' used to be a popular slogan, and we do need the nutrients and minerals like calcium, but dairy products unfortunately also have a considerable amount of sodium. Buy skimmed milk whenever possible, to reduce the fat and calories.

By adding malted milk powder, milk-shake mix, drinking chocolate or cocoa powder to milk, the sodium level is considerably increased to maybe double the natural sodium present in plain milk. Make your own chocolate drink by melting a plain chocolate bar or baking chocolate into a cup of hot milk.

Beers

The sodium in beer will depend in part on the varying proportions of ingredients used to suit regional tastes as well as the sodium content of local water supplies. There are small variations in sodium content from brand to brand, although not between bottles of the same brand. Fortunately, the sodium is generally low, an average of 30mg in a pint. Some scientists have claimed that beer itself has a diuretic effect greater than the consumption of an equivalent amount of water! But the keyword should be moderation!

Spirits

As a general rule, doctors advise a decrease in alcohol consumption to reduce hypertension, so check with your personal physician for any restrictions. Gin, rum, whisky and vodka have 1mg sodium per serving of 2 fl oz. The trouble comes when you add high-sodium mixers to these spirits. Olives or pearl onions garnishing cocktails are taboo for Salt-Watchers.

Wines

Some dietitians suggest a glass of wine with meals because of the higher level of potassium compared to sodium. Readers with severe dietary restrictions should check with their doctors. Generally a 4 fl oz glass of red wine will have 10mg sodium and a glass of white wine will contain about 4mg.

Do not use cooking wine in recipes, as it has a high-salt content, and tonic wine can be high-sodium.

6
What's in the Medicine Cabinet?

Look in your medicine cabinet, and you'll find many drugs and medications containing sodium compounds. These compounds usually make the active ingredient of the medicine more soluble and better absorbed into your system. For instance:

Sodium ampicillin	in antibiotics
Sodium bicarbonate	in antacids
Sodium citrate	in cough medicines
Sodium cloxacillin	in antibiotics
Sodium pentabarbitol	in sedatives (sleeping aids)
Sodium saccharin	in many different medicines
Sodium salicylate	in analgesics (pain-relievers)
Sodium sulphacetamide	in opthalmic (eye) drugs
Sodium sulphosuccinate	in laxatives

If your doctor prescribes medications containing sodium compounds, check with him to ensure they are compatible with a low-sodium diet; also tell your physician of any over-the-counter medicines you use regularly.

Toothpastes

Most standard toothpastes contain minute amounts of sodium generally added to convey fluoride to the dental enamel, to ward off dental caries, or sodium saccharin may be included to give the toothpaste a sweeter taste. Other sodium compounds may be sodium lauryl sulphate, sodium benzoate and sodium silicate. Read the labels for information or write to the manufacturer. It's true these are minute amounts of sodium, measured in parts per million, but it is important to rinse out your mouth thoroughly after brushing your teeth.

Some dentists are advising their patients to use baking soda (bicarbonate of soda) as a dentifrice, but Epsom Salts can be substituted, making a thick paste of 2 tablespoons with hydrogen peroxide. Brush teeth well, and rinse well.

Denture Cleaners and Fixatives

Some of these products may have only traces of sodium, but when cleaners are effervescent they may contain significant quantities of sodium. None of these products is intended to be swallowed, however, and if your dentures are thoroughly rinsed, no sodium will be taken into your system.

Mouthwashes and Gargles

These products may contain sodium. Look at the ingredients label or talk with your pharmacist. Sodium compounds frequently used are sodium phenolate, sodium saccharin, sodium fluoride, sodium benzoate and sodium citrate, sodium lauryl sulphate and disodium editate. Avoid swallowing these products, and rinse with plain tap water afterwards.

Analgesics and Indigestion Remedies

Read the labels. Even simple aspirin can contain a sodium compound. *Boot's Cold Relief* has 39mg of sodium per sachet. An old-fashioned indigestion remedy has been bicarbonate of soda, to be avoided by Salt-Watchers. Generally, effervescent indigestion medicines contain larger amounts of sodium. Here are some examples:

Alka Seltzer	445mg per tablet
Bismag Powder	13,190mg per 100g
Bismag Tablets	41mg per tablet
BiSoDol Powder	15,860mg per 100g
BiSoDol Tablets	17mg per tablet
Boot's Alkaline Stomach Powder	3,425mg per 100g
Boot's Dyspepsia Tablets	41mg per tablet
Boot's Indigestion Mixture	1,235mg per 100g
Boot's Indigestion Tablets	16mg per tablet

Ask your pharmacist or doctor for recommendations on low-sodium alternatives. There are non-prescription remedies on the chemists' shelves with reduced amounts of sodium, or even sodium-free, using aluminium hydroxide or magnesium hydroxide for instance, that can be equally effective.

Laxatives

Many people find that by increasing the fibre in their diet, by eating more fresh fruits and vegetables, whole-grain breads and unprocessed bran, they can improve their regularity and have a decreasing need of laxatives. But if you find them necessary, check with your doctor or pharmacist about the different brands available, and read the labels carefully. Here are a few examples of the sodium content in laxatives on the market:

Andrew's Liver Salt	6,200mg per 100g
Andrew's Liver Salt for diabetics	11,600mg per 100g
Boot's Health Salt	6,400mg per 100g
Boot's Sparkling Health Salt	15,235mg per 100g
Eno's Fruit Salt	15,235mg per 100g
Fynnon Salt	36,035mg per 100g

Vitamin Supplements

Again, read the labels and check different brands and products. Vitamin C may have sodium ascorbate.

7
Software For Salt-Watchers

'Man is a tool-using animal', wrote Thomas Carlyle, the nineteenth century Scottish historian and essayist. 'Without tools he is nothing; with tools he is all.'

To be smart in your shopping, and smart in your eating, you can be quick in your sodium and nutritional accounting with new devices on the market.

Memorable Meals Begin with a Byte

Computers and software are merely the latest of man's tools, and the applications of them for problem-solving appear limitless. A few years ago it would have seemed outlandish to buy your own microcomputer, but prices are falling, and they are now recognized as essential devices in homes as well as organizations, companies, institutions, hospitals and schools. Apart from playing video games, computers can be an educational aid (you can teach as well as learn), and an important tool in keeping the family budget, doing financial planning, helping the children with their homework, and now assisting in achieving good nutrition.

Software seems to capture our imaginations today in the same way that films captured people's imaginations during that industry's formative years. Knowledgeable specialists tell computer buyers first to find the software they want to use, and only then to buy the machine that runs the software. The hardware, software and data must all be compatible since computers are not always interchangeable. The data base is a collection of data put into the computer and retained in the machine's memory.

The software programs usually come on a so-called 'floppy disk' (sometimes called diskettes), a piece of plastic about the size of a single record. They can also be on magnetic tape, or a silicon chip inside a cartridge. Anyone visiting a computer centre, looking at a catalogue, or picking up one of the many computer magazines, can be bewildered by the vast array of products, because as recently as 1980, software was still something of a cottage industry, with programs stuffed into plastic packets and sold mail-order. But the fact is that in Britain, we are more than ever health and diet conscious, and programs are developing increasingly in the fields of nutrition and fitness.

Easy as Pie

If you've got a home computer such as an Apple II, an IBM Personal Computer, or a comparable machine, software is now available that reports on the nutritional values of foods, as well as diet and exercise programs. Some software is designed for use by nutritionists, dietitians in hospitals and weight-reducing spas, but there are programs intended as instruction in schools and for the layperson. It's now possible for a person with high blood-pressure to see, by computer screen, how his hypertension is being affected by a reduction in sodium. Or a family may want to stay within its food budget, but still make sure its meals are nutritionally balanced.

Some programs are based on brand names and others on generic foods. Meals and recipes can be analysed and printouts provided to show the nutrients in food eaten during a certain time, a day, a week. Clearly listed on the printout can be the calories, protein, vitamins and minerals, cholesterol and fat, potassium as well as sodium. Sometimes a summary is given showing trends in eating, and suggestions to help keep within dietary limits. Of course a computer can't do everything for you: it can't tell how often you surreptitiously eat a packet of salty crisps, or open the fridge at night for a snack, nor can it create a meal ready and hot when you come home, but programs have been devised to make out shopping lists, and budget money for the groceries. These programs can increase your awareness of the sodium and other nutrients in individual foods and meals as a whole, improve your diet, and keep you better informed about food.

There are several questions to ask yourself before deciding which software to buy:

1. Do you require a program for analysis of exercise as well as nutrition?
2. Do you need a data base of 4,000 to 6,000 food items for complete accuracy, or will a simpler program be sufficient? Some software has a data base of perhaps only 140 food items, and is more an educational aid for schools.
3. Will the data really fit your requirements? Some displays contain detailed analyses for professionals using technical jargon for nutritionists, while other programs have simpler terms for the busy layperson. Ask for a sample printout from the software company, as well as a manual, to make sure you understand the information provided.
4. Is it easy to input data? If the system is cumbersome, you may find you can't keep up with it on a daily basis.
5. Will you want to store low-sodium recipes?
6. Will you prefer menus developed and shopping lists prepared?
7. Do you want food costs analysed?
8. How much do you want to spend on a program?

A computer has now become the instrument that can help take the mystery and confusion out of nutrition, diet and exercise.

If you are more interested in monitoring your exercise than your diet, some programs can help athletes achieve greater fitness with an aerobics exercise package, evaluating different forms of exercise including jogging, swimming, bicycling, tennis, karate and aerobic dancing.

Here are a few of the software programs available in the nutrition/exercise field. If your local computer centre does not have them in stock, they may be ordered by post. As this is a rapidly growing and changing field of technology, readers should write first to software firms for current catalogues. In the case of US companies, payment should be in US dollars. Ask your bank for an International Money Order drawn on a US bank and payable in US dollars.

B & W *Dietary Analysis*   Price about £250 plus VAT.
Made by: B & W Electronic Systems Ltd, 2 Queen's Place,
         Southsea, Hants PO5 3HF. (Telephone 0705-752702)
Designed for: Commodore 8096 with 2 disk drives, plus Epson
         MX 100 printer.
This program analyses 14 nutrients at once, based on McCance & Widdowson. Also contains a blank disk for recipe storage.

DIETI, DAILYD, EXCHNG, DIETAD and INFODI
         No cost to educational establishments/hospitals.
Made by: School of Nutritional Science, Robert Gordon's Institute
         of Technology, Queen's Road, Aberdeen AB9 2PG.
         (Telephone 0224-633611).
Designed for: DEC 20 mainframe computer, and written in
         COBOL-28.
Five dietary interactive programs, based on McCance & Widdowson, with additional recipes and E products added to data file. DIETI calculates the nutrient content of a meal, recipe or list of foods; DAILYD calculates the nutrient intake for a day, meal by meal; EXCHNG calculates the weights of any selected foods required to obtain any chosen weight of any selected nutrient; DIETAD gives the code numbers and nutrient composition of foods which have been added; INFODI gives the nutrient composition of any food on the file.

H.E.L.P.!   Price upon application to software manufacturer.
Made by: Gate Microsystems Ltd, The Nethergate Centre,
         35 Yeaman Shore, Dundee DD1 4BU.
Designed for: Apple II.
A personal fitness and exercise program for adults, assessing present health and fitness status, and giving advice on modifications in lifestyle towards personal goals and activities.

Microdiet   Price about £85 plus VAT.
Made by: University of Salford, Department of Mathematics
(Mrs. Sallie Bassham, CAMPUS Project Administrator)
The Crescent, Salford M5 4WT.
(Telephone 061-7365843, extension 619 or 682).
Designed for: Sirius, DEC Rainbow 100 or BBC 'B' with 800K disk capacity. Also an earlier version may be used on Superbrain QD and Apple IIe with suitable disk drives.

Microdiet is a dietary analysis program calculating total nutrient intakes and daily averages, using McCance & Widdowson *The Composition of Foods* (4th Edition plus 1980 supplement).

Superdiet   Price about £500 plus VAT.
Made by: Super Software Systems Limited, 'San Michele', Beech Hill Road, Headley, Hants GU35 8DN.
(Telephone 0428-713050).

Designed for: North Star Horizon/Minstrel microcomputer with twin disk drives. Food data file requires capacity of 320K on one disk. For Z80 computers other than North Star Horizon/Minstrel, add £50.

Written in BASIC, by the University of Surrey, this program contains McCance & Widdowson food tables and additional information from the Dunn Nutrition Unit. Program analyses up to 1250 different foods with over 100 nutritional constituents. Diets can be analysed by meal, day or number of days, in detail or in summary. Diets can be filed and recalled later.

Chubby Checker   Price about $95.
Made by: Medical Logic International, 5 Pathfinder Drive, Sumter, SC 29150, USA.
Designed for: HP-85, Series 80, 82903A memory Module.

A food and total calorie program, not nutritional analysis. Data base of 330 foods. Will calculate calories consumed and project weight gain/loss if same calorie level is maintained.

Computer Chef   Price about $50.
Made by: Norell Data Systems Corp., 3400 Wilshire Boulevard, P.O. Box 70127, Los Angeles, CA 90010, USA.
Designed for: IBM PC or compatible. PC-DOS version 1.1 or 2.2 64K RAM. One single-sided double-density disk drive. Printer.

Stores recipes. Amounts of individual ingredients can be changed by the computer to produce the number of servings needed. Computerized cookery book and recipe file.

The DINE System   Price about $80.
Made by: The DINE System, 724 Robin Road, West Amherst,
         NY 14228, USA.
Designed for: Franklin Ace 1000; PET with Apple emulator;
         Apple II (48K), Apple III, Apple IIe; IBM PC.
3 diskettes (DINE disk, Food disk A, and Food disk B). Provides actual calories of selected foods and amounts of protein, fats, complex carbohydrates, sugar, cholesterol, vitamin C, sodium and iron. Dietary guidelines based upon personal input data. Tracks alcohol consumption. Data base of 3300+ food codes.

Eat Smart   Price about $20.
Made by: The Pillsbury Company, (Eat Smart Kit M/S 3286),
         Pillsbury Center, Minneapolis, MN 55402, USA.
Designed for: Apple II (48K), DOS 3.3, Apple IIe, Apple III.
         With or without a printer.
An educational tool. Data base of 136 foods. Analyses diet daily, calculating percentage of (US) Recommended Daily Allowances met (eight key nutrients) and suggests improvements in diet.

Health-Aide   Price about $80.
Made by: Programming Technology Corporation, 7 San Marcos
         Place, San Rafael, CA 94901, USA.
Designed for: Apple II, II+, IIe, III, (48K), DOS 3.3;
         IBM PC (128K) DOS 2.0.
With an expandable data base of over 800 foods for 37 nutrients, foods are analysed, cost analysed, blood-pressure monitored. Provides 21 balanced menus for different calorie levels, makes shopping lists. Energy expenditures calculated through time spent each day on 150 different activities. (Other diskettes are available from this company offering a recipes file and further menus.)

Nutri-Calc   Price about $129.
Made by: PCD Systems, Inc., P.O. Box 277, 163 Main Street,
         Penn Yan, NY 14527, USA.

Designed for: Apple, Apple II+ (48K Min. and 2 disk drives), Apple IIe, Apple III (an Apple emulation mode); IBM PC and XT; Columbia MPC; Sage; Altos 8000 Series (64K Min.); IBM Displaywriter, and CP/M based computers with 8-inch (20cm) disk drives and at least 48K RAM.

Data base of 900 foods with 18 common nutrients per food. Extra spaces for 100 extra foods of your choice. Fast, accurate analyses of diet, menus and recipes. Calculations of ideal weight and caloric consumption. Can set up schedule for weight loss/gain. Can customize recipes and menus for up to seven days.

Nutritionist 1 Price about $145.
Made by: N-Squared Computing, 5318 Forest Ridge Road,
   Silverton, OR 97381, USA.
Designed for: Apple II+ (48K RAM) DOS 3.3, 1 disk drive;
   IBM PC (64K RAM) 1 disk drive.

An expandable data base of 730 foods analysing 19 nutrients. Can analyse single foods, recipes, entire meals, daily menus and complete diets. Can calculate optimum caloric intake on an individual basis depending on activity level.

Food/Fluids Price about $295.
Made by: Medical Logic International, 5 Pathfinder Drive,
   Sumter, SC 29150, USA.
Designed for: HP-85, Series 80, 82903A Memory Module.

Two programs to assist the physician and his clinical team in determining the appropriateness of food and fluids, appraising quantity and content. Printout of calories, protein, fats and carbohydrates. Display shows actual consumption versus goal consumption and projects weight, one year hence. With fluid balance assessment, the correctness of a patient's body water load is given, osmolar concentration and acid-base relationship. Printout summarizes fluid problems, describing necessary replacements useful for return to physiological homeostasis.

Nutriplanner-800 and *Nutriplanner*-1600   Price about $664 each.
Made by: Practorcare, 10951 Sorrento Valley Road, Suite-II-F,
   San Diego, CA 92121, USA.

Designed for: Apple IIe (128K RAM); IBM PC; 2 floppy disk drives, 12-inch (30cm) video monitor.

The 1600 system is especially for dietitians, physicians and food service managers, with a data base of up to 1600 food and formula items. The 800 system, with data base of 800 foods, 25 nutrient components and six food exchanges, can assess diet, analyse recipes, store recipes and patient data, and provide an analysis of food costs and monthly food budget.

If you don't have a personal home computer, there are other machines to help Salt-Watchers, for instance: *Compucal* which is a computerized diet/kitchen scale, available from quality kitchen-supply shops. It's made in Scotland and distributed throughout the UK and is also on sale in Bamix shops in Australia. This 9×7 inch (23×18cm) device works on six C-size batteries or, with a 9-volt adaptor, on house current. *Compucal* gives you a digital readout of the weight of food portions in ounces or grams, with the sodium, calories, protein, carbohydrates, fats and cholesterol.

Now it's all at your fingertips! See how sodium adds up!
There are many ways to cut salt and sodium.
Start now to be a Salt-Watcher!

Appendix I
The Sodium Content of Your Food

Food or Drink	Quantity	Approx. portion	Sodium (mg)
BEVERAGES:			
Alcoholic:			
Beers:			
Brown ale, bottled	275ml	½ pt	44
Bitter: canned	275ml	½ pt	25
draught	275ml	½ pt	33
keg	275ml	½ pt	22
Lager, bottled	275ml	½ pt	11
Mild, draught	275ml	½ pt	30
Pale ale, bottled	275ml	½ pt	27
Stout, bottled	275ml	½ pt	63
Stout extra	275ml	½ pt	11
Strong ale	275ml	½ pt	41
Ciders:			
Dry or sweet	275ml	½ pt	19
Vintage	275ml	½ pt	6
Spirits:			
Gin, rum, whisky, vodka	60ml	2 fl oz	1
Wines:			
Red (Burgundy, Beaujolais, Claret)	100ml	4 fl oz	10
Rosé, medium	100ml	4 fl oz	4

Food or Drink	Quantity	Approx. portion	Sodium (mg)
BEVERAGES (continued):			
White: Dry	100ml	4 fl oz	4
Medium (Graves)	100ml	4 fl oz	21
Sweet (Sauternes)	100ml	4 fl oz	13
Sparkling (Champagne)	100ml	4 fl oz	4
Port	100ml	4 fl oz	4
Sherries: Dry	100ml	4 fl oz	10
Medium	100ml	4 fl oz	6
Sweet	100ml	4 fl oz	13
Tonic wine (Phospherine)	100ml	4 fl oz	124
Vermouth: Dry	100ml	4 fl oz	17
Sweet	100ml	4 fl oz	28
Beef and vegetable extracts:			
Bovril		1 cup	1465
Bovril beef cube		1 cube	1890
Bovril chicken cube		1 cube	2080
Marmite		1 cup	458
Oxo beef drink		1 tsp	280
Coffee and tea:			
Coffee, infusion	170ml	6 fl oz	Tr.
Coffee, instant	170ml	6 fl oz	Tr.
Coffee, concentrated essence	15ml	1 tbsp	10
Tea, infusion	170ml	6 fl oz	Tr.
Fruit drinks, fruit juices, soft drinks:			
Apple juice	100ml	4 fl oz	8
Blackcurrant (Ribena), concentrated	30ml	1 fl oz	7

Food or Drink	Quantity	Approx. portion	Sodium (mg)
BEVERAGES (continued):			
Coca Cola	100ml	4 fl oz	8
Coconut milk	100ml	4 fl oz	110
Ginger ale	100ml	4 fl oz	5
Grapefruit juice, canned	100ml	4 fl oz	3
Lemonade, bottled	100ml	4 fl oz	7
Lemon juice, fresh	100ml	4 fl oz	2
bottled, comminuted (average)	100ml	4 fl oz	35
Lemon squash, undiluted, comm. (average)	30ml	1 fl oz	12
Lime juice cordial, undiluted	30ml	1 fl oz	2
Lucozade	100ml	4 fl oz	30
Orange drink, undiluted	30ml	1 fl oz	6
Orange juice,			
fresh squeezed	100ml	4 fl oz	2
canned	100ml	4 fl oz	4
frozen, diluted	100ml	4 fl oz	2
Pineapple juice, canned	100ml	4 fl oz	1
Pomegranate juice	100ml	4 fl oz	1
Prune juice	100ml	4 fl oz	2
Ribena (blackcurrant), undiluted	30ml	1 fl oz	7
Rosehip syrup, undiluted	30ml	1 fl oz	84
Soda water (average)	100ml	4 fl oz	28
Tomato juice, canned	100ml	4 fl oz	240
Tonic water (average)	100ml	4 fl oz	3
Tonic water, low-calorie	100ml	4 fl oz	14

Food or Drink	Quantity	Approx. portion	Sodium (mg)
BEVERAGES (continued):			
Milk, milk drinks, chocolate drinks:			
Cow's: fresh, whole	275ml	½ pt	150
fresh, skimmed	275ml	½ pt	156
sterilized or longlife	275ml	½ pt	150
condensed, whole	140ml	¼ pt	234
condensed, skimmed	140ml	¼ pt	324
evaporated, whole, unsweetened	140ml	¼ pt	270
dried, whole	50g	2 oz	220
dried, skimmed	50g	2 oz	275
Goat's milk	100g	3½ oz	40
Human milk (10 days after birth)	100g	3½ oz	48
Human milk (1 month after birth)	100g	3½ oz	14
Bournvita	15g	2 tbsp	69
Cocoa powder	15g	2 tbsp	142
Drinking chocolate	15g	2 tbsp	37
Malted milk (*Horlicks*)	15g	2 tbsp	49
Malted milk (*Horlicks*), instant	15g	2 tbsp	96
Non-dairy coffee or tea whitener (average)	6g	1 tbsp	10
Ovaltine	15g	2 tbsp	16

Food or Drink	Quantity	Approx. portion	Sodium (mg)
BISCUITS:			
Chocolate, full coated	25g	2 biscuits	40
Chocolate chip	25g	2 biscuits	76
Cream crackers (average)	25g	2 biscuits	152
Crispbread, rye	25g	2 biscuits	55
rye, brown	25g	2 biscuits	110
wheat, starch-reduced	25g	2 biscuits	152
wheat, unsalted	25g	2 biscuits	1
Digestive, plain	25g	2 biscuits	110
chocolate	25g	2 biscuits	112
Fig rolls	25g	2 biscuits	70
Gingernuts	25g	2 biscuits	82
Matzohs	25g	2 biscuits	4
Oatcakes	25g	2 biscuits	307
Sandwich	25g	2 biscuits	55
Semi-sweet	25g	2 biscuits	102
Shortcake	25g	2 biscuits	90
Wafers, filled	25g	2 biscuits	17
Water	25g	2 biscuits	117
BREADS:			
Brown, average	25g	1 slice	137
Hovis	25g	1 slice	145
Chapatis (made with fat)	25g	1 chapati	32
Currant	25g	1 slice	40
Malt	25g	1 slice	70
Pumpernickel (average) (U.S. figures)	25g	1 slice	172
Soda	25g	1 slice	102
White, average	25g	1 slice	135
low-sodium (canned)	25g	1 slice	2
Wholemeal	25g	1 slice	135

Food or Drink	Quantity	Approx. portion	Sodium (mg)
BREAKFAST CEREALS:			
All-Bran	25g	1 oz	382
Bemax (wheat germ)	25g	1 oz	1
Bran, natural wheat	25g	1 oz	7
Bran Flakes (average)	25g	1 oz	235
Corn Flakes	25g	1 oz	295
Grapenuts (average)	25g	1 oz	165
Muesli, commercial (average)	25g	1 oz	45
Oatmeal, raw	25g	1 oz	8
Puffed Wheat (average)	25g	1 oz	1
Ready Brek	25g	1 oz	10
Rice Krispies	25g	1 oz	282
Shredded Wheat	25g	1 biscuit	3
Shreddies	25g	1 oz	142
Special K	25g	1 oz	245
Sugar Puffs	25g	1 oz	2
Sultana Bran	25g	1 oz	177
Weetabix	25g	1 oz	94
BUNS AND PASTRIES:			
Crumpets, commercial	25g	1 crumpet	205
Currant buns, commercial	25g	1 bun	25
Doughnuts, commercial	25g	1 doughnut	15
Eclairs, commercial	25g	1 éclair	40
Jam tarts, commercial	25g	1 tart	57
Mince pies, commercial	25g	1 pie	85
Muffins, commercial	25g	1 muffin	55
Scones, commercial	25g	1 scone	135
Scotch pancakes, commercial	25g	1 pancake	67

Food or Drink	Quantity	Approx. portion	Sodium (mg)
CAKES:			
Fancy iced cakes, commercial (average)	50g	1 slice	125
Fruit cake, commercial (average)	50g	1 slice	120
Ginger cake, commercial (average)	50g	1 slice	245
Madeira, commercial (average)	50g	1 slice	190
Rock cakes, standard home-made recipe	50g	2 cakes	240
Sponge, without fat, standard home-made recipe	50g	1 slice	41
Swiss-roll, commercial (average)	50g	1 slice	210
Victoria sponge, commercial (average)	50g	1 slice	175
DAIRY PRODUCTS:			
Butter:			
salted (average)	25g	1 oz	217
unsalted	25g	1 oz	2
Cheeses:			
Brie	25g	1 oz	159
Caerphilly	25g	1 oz	102
Camembert	25g	1 oz	352
Cheddar (average)	25g	1 oz	188
Cheese spread	25g	1 oz	292
Cheshire (average)	25g	1 oz	135
Cottage	100g	3½ oz	450
Cream cheese	25g	1 oz	75
Danish Blue	25g	1 oz	355
Derbyshire	25g	1 oz	142

Food or Drink	Quantity	Approx. portion	Sodium (mg)
DAIRY PRODUCTS (continued):			
Double Gloucester	25g	1 oz	142
Edam	25g	1 oz	245
Féta	25g	1 oz	282
Gorgonzola	25g	1 oz	350
Gouda	25g	1 oz	207
Lancashire	25g	1 oz	147
Leicester	25g	1 oz	155
Limburger	25g	1 oz	203
Mozzarella (from skimmed milk)	25g	1 oz	200
Neufchatel	25g	1 oz	101
Parmesan	25g	1 oz	190
Processed	25g	1 oz	340
Provolone	25g	1 oz	221
Ricotta (from skimmed milk)	100g	3½ oz	125
Roquefort	25g	1 oz	458
Stilton, blue	25g	1 oz	287
white	25g	1 oz	187
Swiss (Emmenthal)	25g	1 oz	66
Tilsit	25g	1 oz	190
Wensleydale	25g	1 oz	112
Cream:			
double	25g	2 tbsp	7
single, fresh	25g	2 tbsp	10
soured commercially, fresh	25g	2 tbsp	10
sterilized, canned	25g	2 tbsp	14
whipping	25g	2 tbsp	8

Food or Drink	Quantity	Approx. portion	Sodium (mg)
DAIRY PRODUCTS (continued):			
Milk:			
Cow's: fresh, whole	275ml	½ pt	150
fresh, skimmed	275ml	½ pt	156
sterilized or longlife	275ml	½ pt	150
condensed, whole	140ml	¼ pt	234
condensed, skimmed	140ml	¼ pt	324
evaporated, whole unsweetened	140ml	¼ pt	270
dried, whole	50g	2 oz	220
dried, skimmed	50g	2 oz	275
Goat's milk	100g	3½ oz	40
Human milk (10 days after birth)	100g	3½ oz	48
Human milk (1 month after birth)	100g	3½ oz	14
Yogurt:			
flavoured (average)	100g	3½ oz	64
fruit (average)	100g	3½ oz	64
hazelnut	100g	3½ oz	70
natural (average)	100g	3½ oz	76
EGGS:			
Whole	50g	1 egg	70
Yolk	17g	1 yolk	8
White	33g	1 white	62
Dried	50g	2 oz	260

Food or Drink	Quantity	Approx. portion	Sodium (mg)
FATS, MARGARINES AND OILS:			
Cod liver oil	100g	3½ oz	Tr.
Cooking fat	100g	3½ oz	Tr.
Dripping (beef)	100g	3½ oz	5
Lard	100g	3½ oz	2
Low-fat spread, salted (average)	15g	1 tbsp	103
Margarine, salted (average)	15g	1 tbsp	120
Suet, block	100g	3½ oz	21
shredded	100g	3½ oz	Tr.
Vegetable oils	15g	1 tbsp	Tr.
FISH AND SHELLFISH:			
Fish and fish products:			
Bloater, grilled	85g	3 oz	595
Cod, raw	85g	3 oz	65
fried in batter	85g	3 oz	85
poached	85g	3 oz	93
smoked, poached	85g	3 oz	1020
dried, salted, boiled	85g	3 oz	340
Cod roe, fried	50g	2 oz	65
Coley (saithe), raw	85g	3 oz	62
steamed	85g	3 oz	82
Dogfish (rock salmon), fried in batter	85g	3 oz	246
Eel, raw	85g	3 oz	76
Fish cakes, frozen (average)	85g	3 oz	408
Fish fingers, frozen (average)	85g	3 oz	272
Fish paste	25g	1 oz	150

Food or Drink	Quantity	Approx. portion	Sodium (mg)
FISH AND SHELLFISH (continued):			
Haddock, fresh, raw	85g	3 oz	102
fried	85g	3 oz	153
smoked, steamed	85g	3 oz	1037
Halibut, fresh, raw	85g	3 oz	71
steamed	85g	3 oz	93
Herring, fresh, raw	85g	3 oz	57
fried	85g	3 oz	85
pickled (roll-mop)	85g	3 oz	1445
Herring roe, fried	50g	2 oz	44
Kedgeree, home-made	85g	3 oz	671
Kipper, baked	85g	3 oz	841
Lemon sole, fresh, raw	85g	3 oz	81
steamed	85g	3 oz	102
fried	85g	3 oz	119
Mackerel, fresh, raw	85g	3 oz	110
fried	85g	3 oz	127
Pilchards, canned in tomato sauce	85g	3 oz	314
Plaice, fresh, raw or steamed	85g	3 oz	102
fried in batter	85g	3 oz	187
Rock salmon (dogfish) fried in batter	85g	3 oz	246
Salmon, fresh, raw	85g	3 oz	83
steamed	85g	3 oz	93
canned	85g	3 oz	484
smoked	85g	3 oz	1598
Sardines, canned in oil (fish only)	50g	2 oz	325
canned in tomato sauce	50g	2 oz	350

Food or Drink	Quantity	Approx. portion	Sodium (mg)
FISH AND SHELLFISH (continued):			
Skate, fried in batter	85g	3 oz	119
Sprats, fried	85g	3 oz	110
Trout, brown river,			
steamed	85g	3 oz	75
sea, steamed	85g	3 oz	178
Tuna, canned in oil	85g	3 oz	357
Whitebait, fried	85g	3 oz	195
Whiting, fried	85g	3 oz	170
steamed	85g	3 oz	110
Shellfish:			
Cockles, boiled (no shells)	85g	3 oz	2992
Crab, boiled (no shell)	85g	3 oz	314
canned	85g	3 oz	467
Lobster, boiled (no shell)	85g	3 oz	280
Mussels, raw	85g	3 oz	246
boiled	85g	3 oz	178
canned	85g	3 oz	401
Oysters, raw (no shells)	85g	3 oz	433
Prawns, boiled in sea-water (no shells)	85g	3 oz	1351
Scallops, steamed (no shells)	85g	3 oz	229
Scampi, frozen, fried	85g	3 oz	323
Shrimps, boiled (no shells)	85g	3 oz	3264
canned	85g	3 oz	833
Whelks, boiled in sea-water (no shells)	85g	3 oz	229
Winkles, boiled in sea-water (no shells)	85g	3 oz	969

Food or Drink	Quantity	Approx. portion	Sodium (mg)
FLOURS, GRAINS AND STARCHES:			
Arrowroot	25g	1 oz	1
Bran, soya (gluten free)	25g	1 oz	5
wheat, natural unprocessed	25g	1 oz	7
Cornflour	25g	1 oz	13
Custard powder	25g	1 oz	80
Dumpling mix, commercial	100g	3½ oz	650
Flour:			
breadmaking, white	100g	3½ oz	3
brown (85 per cent)	100g	3½ oz	4
plain, white	100g	3½ oz	2
rye	100g	3½ oz	1
self-raising, white	100g	3½ oz	350
soya	100g	3½ oz	1
wholemeal (100 per cent)	100g	3½ oz	3
Macaroni, raw	100g	3½ oz	26
Macaroni cheese, commercial	100g	3½ oz	605
Oatmeal, raw	25g	1 oz	8
Pastry, puff, frozen, commercial	100g	3½ oz	550
short-crust, frozen, commercial	100g	3½ oz	390
short-crust mix, commercial	100g	3½ oz	570
Pearl barley	25g	1 oz	1
Ravioli, canned in tomato sauce	100g	3½ oz	715
Rice, raw	100g	3½ oz	6
savoury, commercial (average)	100g	3½ oz	470

Food or Drink	Quantity	Approx. portion	Sodium (mg)
FLOURS, GRAINS AND STARCHES (continued):			
canned pudding, commercial (average)	100g	3½ oz	50
Sago, raw	100g	3½ oz	3
Semolina, raw	100g	3½ oz	12
pudding, canned	100g	3½ oz	62
Spaghetti, raw	100g	3½ oz	5
bolognese, canned	100g	3½ oz	410
canned in tomato sauce	100g	3½ oz	500
Tapioca, raw	100g	3½ oz	4
Wheat germ (Bemax)	25g	1 oz	1
FRUITS:			
Apples, raw	100g	1 apple	2
dried, commercial	100g	3½ oz	88
Apple sauce, canned	50g	2 oz	2
dry mix	50g	2 oz	900
Apricots, raw	100g	3 apricots	1
canned	100g	3½ oz	1
dried, commercial	100g	3½ oz	56
Avocado pears	200g	1 avocado	4
Bananas, raw	100g	1 banana	1
Bilberries, fresh or frozen	100g	3½ oz	1
Blackberries, raw	100g	3½ oz	4
Blackcurrants, stewed with sugar	100g	3½ oz	2
Blueberries, canned	100g	3½ oz	1

Food or Drink	Quantity	Approx. portion	Sodium (mg)
FRUITS (continued):			
Cherries, cooking, stewed without sugar	100g	3½ oz	3
eating, raw	100g	3½ oz	3
glacé	25g	1 oz	16
Cranberries, raw	100g	3½ oz	2
Cranberry sauce, jellied, commercial	50g	2 oz	14
Currants, dried	100g	3½ oz	20
Damsons, raw or stewed	100g	3 damsons	2
Dates, dried	50g	6 dates	2
Figs, raw	100g	2 figs	2
dried, commercial	100g	5 figs	87
Fruit-pie filling, canned	100g	3½ oz	30
Fruit salad, canned	100g	3½ oz	2
Gooseberries, raw or stewed with sugar	100g	3½ oz	2
Grapes, black or white	50g	10 grapes	1
Grapefruit, raw	100g	½ fruit	1
canned, sweetened	100g	3½ oz	10
Greengages, raw or stewed	100g	3 gages	1
Guavas, canned	100g	3½ oz	7
Kumquats	100g	5 kumquats	5
Lemons, whole	100g	1 lemon	6
Limes, whole	50g	1 lime	1
Loganberries, raw or stewed	100g	3½ oz	3
canned	100g	3½ oz	1
Lychees, raw	100g	3½ oz	3
canned	100g	3½ oz	2
Mandarins, canned	100g	3½ oz	9

Food or Drink	Quantity	Approx. portion	Sodium (mg)
FRUITS (continued):			
Mangoes, raw	200g	1 mango	14
canned	100g	3½ oz	3
Medlars	100g	3½ oz	6
Melons, cantaloup	270g	½ melon	24
honeydew	300g	⅕ melon	36
watermelon	400g	¹⁄₁₆ melon	8
Mulberries, raw	100g	3½ oz	2
Nectarines, raw	120g	1 nectarine	10
Olives, in brine (without stones)	25g	4 olives	562
Oranges, raw, whole	100g	1 orange	2
juice only	100ml	4 fl oz	2
Passionfruit, raw	100g	3½ oz	28
Pawpaw, fresh	150g	½ pawpaw	4
canned	100g	3½ oz	8
Peaches, fresh, whole	100g	1 peach	2
canned	100g	3½ oz	1
dried	100g	3½ oz	6
Pears, eating, whole	100g	1 pear	1
cooking, stewed with sugar	100g	3½ oz	2
canned	100g	3½ oz	1
Pineapple, fresh	100g	3½ oz	2
canned	100g	3½ oz	1
Plums, Victoria, fresh or cooking, stewed	100g	2 plums	2
Prunes, dried, raw	50g	6 prunes	6
stewed without sugar	50g	6 prunes	3
Quinces, raw	100g	3½ oz	3
Raisins, dried	100g	3½ oz	52

Food or Drink	Quantity	Approx. portion	Sodium (mg)
FRUITS (continued):			
Raspberries, raw or stewed	100g	3½ oz	3
canned	100g	3½ oz	4
Redcurrants, raw or stewed with sugar	100g	3½ oz	2
Rhubarb, raw or stewed with sugar	100g	3½ oz	2
Strawberries, raw	100g	10 berries	2
canned	100g	3½ oz	7
Sultanas, dried	100g	3½ oz	53
Tangeloes	100g	1 tangelo	1
Tangerines, raw	85g	1 tangerine	1
MEATS:			
Bacon:			
back rasher, grilled	25g	1 oz	505
collar joint, boiled	85g	3 oz	935
gammon joint, boiled	85g	3 oz	816
gammon rasher, grilled	25g	1 oz	535
middle rasher, grilled	25g	1 oz	500
streaky rasher, grilled	25g	1 oz	497
Beef:			
dressed carcass, raw	85g	3 oz	47
beefburgers, frozen, fried	100g	3½ oz	880
beef pies, frozen, commercial	100g	3½ oz	733
beef sausages, grilled	85g	3 oz	935
brisket, raw	85g	3 oz	58
corned beef, canned	85g	3 oz	807
mince, raw	85g	3 oz	73
rumpsteak, raw	85g	3 oz	43
grilled	85g	3 oz	47

Food or Drink	Quantity	Approx. portion	Sodium (mg)
MEATS (continued):			
silverside, salted, boiled	85g	3 oz	773
sirloin, raw	85g	3 oz	42
roast	85g	3 oz	46
stewing steak, raw	85g	3 oz	61
canned, with gravy	85g	3 oz	323
topside, raw	85g	3 oz	37
roast	85g	3 oz	41
Lamb:			
dressed carcass, raw	85g	3 oz	60
breast, raw	85g	3 oz	85
roasted	85g	3 oz	62
chops, raw	85g	3 oz	52
grilled	85g	3 oz	61
leg, raw	85g	3 oz	44
roasted	85g	3 oz	55
scrag and neck, raw	85g	3 oz	60
shoulder, raw	85g	3 oz	56
roasted	85g	3 oz	52
Offal and offal products:			
Black pudding, fried	85g	3 oz	1028
Brains, calf or lamb, raw	85g	3 oz	119
Faggots	85g	3 oz	697
Haggis, boiled	85g	3 oz	654
Heart, lamb, raw	85g	3 oz	119
ox, raw	85g	3 oz	81
pig, raw	85g	3 oz	68
Kidney, lamb, raw	85g	3 oz	187
ox, raw	85g	3 oz	153
pig, raw	85g	3 oz	161

Food or Drink	Quantity	Approx. portion	Sodium (mg)
MEATS (continued):			
Liver, calf, raw	85g	3 oz	79
chicken, raw	85g	3 oz	72
lamb, raw	85g	3 oz	65
ox, raw	85g	3 oz	69
pig, raw	85g	3 oz	74
Liver sausage	50g	2 oz	430
Oxtail, raw	85g	3 oz	93
Sweetbread, lamb, raw	85g	3 oz	64
Tongue, lamb, raw	85g	3 oz	357
sheep, stewed	85g	3 oz	68
ox, pickled,			
raw	85g	3 oz	1028
canned	85g	3 oz	892
Tripe, dressed	85g	3 oz	39
Pork:			
dressed carcass, raw	85g	3 oz	55
bellyrashers, grilled	25g	1 oz	24
ham, canned	85g	3 oz	1062
leg, raw	85g	3 oz	50
roasted	85g	3 oz	67
loinchops, raw	85g	3 oz	48
grilled	85g	3 oz	71
pork pie, individual	100g	3½ oz	720
sausages, pork, grilled	85g	3 oz	850
Sausages:			
beef, grilled	85g	3 oz	935
pork, grilled	85g	3 oz	850
frankfurter	50g	1 sausage	490
polony	50g	2 oz	435
salami	50g	2 slices	925
saveloy	50g	2 oz	445
white pudding	50g	2 oz	185

Food or Drink	Quantity	Approx. portion	Sodium (mg)
MEATS (continued):			
Veal:			
cutlet, fried	85g	3 oz	93
fillet, roast	85g	3 oz	82
jellied, canned	85g	3 oz	1011
Other meat products:			
Beef stock cube (Bovril)		1 cube	1890
Brawn	50g	2 slices	375
Corned beef, canned	85g	3 oz	807
Cornish pastie, commercial (average)	100g	3½ oz	590
Ham and pork, chopped, canned	50g	2 slices	545
Liver sausage	50g	2 oz	430
Luncheon meat, canned	50g	2 oz	525
Meat paste	25g	1 oz	185
Pork pie, individual, commercial (average)	100g	3½ oz	720
Sausage roll, commercial (average)	85g	3 oz	494
Steak and kidney pie, commercial (average)	100g	3½ oz	510
Stewed steak with gravy, canned	85g	3 oz	323
Tongue, canned	85g	3 oz	892
Veal, jellied, canned	85g	3 oz	1011

Food or Drink	Quantity	Approx. portion	Sodium (mg)
NUTS:			
Almonds, shelled, raw	100g	3½ oz	6
shelled, roasted, salted	100g	3½ oz	198
Almond paste (marzipan)	100g	3½ oz	13
Barcelona nuts	100g	3½ oz	3
Brazil nuts	100g	3½ oz	2
Cashews, fresh, raw	100g	3½ oz	14
roasted, salted	100g	3½ oz	580
Chestnuts	100g	3½ oz	11
Coconut, fresh	100g	3½ oz	17
desiccated	100g	3½ oz	28
Hazelnuts (cob nuts)	100g	3½ oz	1
Mixed nuts, roasted, salted, commercial (average)	100g	3½ oz	500
Peanuts, fresh, raw	100g	3½ oz	6
roasted, salted	100g	3½ oz	440
Peanut butter	30g	2 tbsp	105
Pistachios, fresh, shelled	100g	3½ oz	5
salted	100g	3½ oz	112
Walnuts, fresh, shelled	100g	3½ oz	3
pickled, commercial (average)	25g	1 oz	270

Food or Drink	Quantity	Approx. portion	Sodium (mg)
POULTRY AND GAME:			
Chicken:			
raw, meat only	85g	3 oz	69
boiled, meat only	85g	3 oz	70
roast, meat only	85g	3 oz	69
wing quarter	85g	3 oz	35
leg quarter	85g	3 oz	42
liver, fried	85g	3 oz	204
Turkey:			
raw, meat only	85g	3 oz	46
roast, dark meat	85g	3 oz	60
roast, light meat	85g	3 oz	38
Game:			
Duck, raw, meat only	85g	3 oz	93
roast, meat only	85g	3 oz	82
Goose, roast, meat only	85g	3 oz	127
Grouse, roast, meat only	85g	3 oz	82
Hare, stewed, meat only	85g	3 oz	34
Partridge, roast, meat only	85g	3 oz	85
Pheasant, roast, meat only	85g	3 oz	85
Pigeon, roast, meat only	85g	3 oz	93
Rabbit, raw, meat only	85g	3 oz	57
stewed	85g	3 oz	27
Venison, roast, meat only	85g	3 oz	73

Food or Drink	Quantity	Approx. portion	Sodium (mg)
PRESERVES AND SPREADS:			
Fish paste	20g	1 tbsp	120
Honey	20g	1 tbsp	2
Jam, from berries and currants	20g	1 tbsp	3
from stoned fruits	20g	1 tbsp	2
Lemon curd, starch base	20g	1 tbsp	13
Marmalade, commercial (average)	20g	1 tbsp	4
Marmite	10g	1 tsp	458
Meat paste	20g	1 tbsp	148
Mincemeat, commercial (average)	100g	3½ oz	140
Peanut butter	30g	2 tbsp	105
Sandwich spread	25g	1 oz	250
Syrup, golden	20g	1 tbsp	54
maple, pure	20g	1 tbsp	1
maple, imitation	20g	1 tbsp	20
Treacle, black	20g	1 tbsp	19
PUDDINGS AND DESSERTS:			
Apple pie, commercial	85g	3 oz	78
Cheesecake, commercial	25g	1 oz	75
Fruit pie, individual, commercial	85g	3 oz	178
Ice-cream, dairy	85g	3 oz	68
non-dairy	85g	3 oz	59
Jelly, packet cubes	100g	3½ oz	25
Milk pudding with rice, canned	100g	3½ oz	50
Semolina pudding, commercial	100g	3½ oz	62
Sponge pudding, canned, chocolate	50g	2 oz	125
mixed fruit	50g	2 oz	167
treacle	50g	2 oz	175

Food or Drink	Quantity	Approx. portion	Sodium (mg)
SAUCES, PICKLES AND CONDIMENTS:			
Brown sauce, bottled	15g	1 tbsp	147
low-sodium	15g	1 tbsp	9
Cabbage, red, pickled, commercial	25g	1 oz	212
Capers, pickled	25g	1 oz	450
Cranberry sauce, jellied, commercial	50g	2 oz	14
French dressing, commercial	15g	1 tbsp	114
Gravy concentrate, commercial	15g	1 tbsp	675
Horseradish, raw	15g	1 tbsp	1
Horseradish sauce, commercial	15g	1 tbsp	60
low-sodium	15g	1 tbsp	4
Mayonnaise, commercial	15g	1 tbsp	144
low-sodium	15g	1 tbsp	3
Mustard pickle, commercial	15g	1 tbsp	175
Mustard powder	5g	1 tsp	2
Mustard, prepared, American	15g	1 tbsp	195
Dijon	15g	1 tbsp	585
English	15g	1 tbsp	510
English, low-sodium	15g	1 tbsp	4
French, low-sodium	15g	1 tbsp	4
Olives, in brine, without stones	25g	4 olives	562
Onions, pickled	25g	1 onion	175
silverskin	15g	1 onion	131
Pepper, black or white	2g	1 tsp	Tr.
Piccalilli	15g	1 tbsp	164

Food or Drink	Quantity	Approx. portion	Sodium (mg)
SAUCES, PICKLES AND CONDIMENTS (continued):			
Pickle, sweet	15g	1 tbsp	255
Salad cream, commercial	15g	1 tbsp	180
low-sodium	15g	1 tbsp	3
Salt, celery	5g	1 tsp	1456
garlic	5g	1 tsp	1456
onion	5g	1 tsp	1455
Salt, table	5g	1 tsp	1942
Salt-substitute, low-sodium (average)	5g	1 tsp	971
sodium-free	5g	1 tsp	Tr.
Sandwich spread, commercial	25g	1 oz	250
Soya sauce	20g	1 tbsp	1468
Tartar sauce, commercial	15g	1 tbsp	120
low-sodium	15g	1 tbsp	4
Tomato ketchup (tomato sauce)	15g	1 tbsp	217
low-sodium, commercial	15g	1 tbsp	9
Tomato sauce (for cooking)	100g	3½ oz	850
Vinegar	15g	1 tbsp	3
Walnuts, pickled, commercial	25g	1 oz	270
Worcestershire sauce	15g	1 tbsp	195
low-sodium	15g	1 tbsp	4

Food or Drink	Quantity	Approx. portion	Sodium (mg)
SOUPS:			
Beef Broth, canned, ready to serve	240g	8 fl oz	1224
Beef Soup, canned, ready to serve	240g	8 fl oz	1608
Celery, Cream of, canned, ready to serve	240g	8 fl oz	1248
low-calorie	240g	8 fl oz	1200
Celery, dried, low-sodium, as served	240g	8 fl oz	20
Chicken, Cream of, canned, ready to serve	240g	8 fl oz	1104
Chicken, condensed, as served	240g	8 fl oz	840
Chicken, canned, low-calorie	240g	8 fl oz	1248
Chicken Noodle, dried, as served	240g	8 fl oz	888
Golden Chicken and Mushroom, ready to serve	240g	8 fl oz	1728
Golden Chicken and Vegetable, ready to serve	240g	8 fl oz	1920
Lentil canned, ready to serve	240g	8 fl oz	1248
Minestrone, dried, as served	240g	8 fl oz	1032
Mulligatawny, canned, ready to serve	240g	8 fl oz	1116
Mushroom, Cream of, canned, ready to serve	240g	8 fl oz	1128
Mushroom, dried, low-sodium, as served	240g	8 fl oz	20

Food or Drink	Quantity	Approx. portion	Sodium (mg)
SOUPS (continued):			
Oxtail, canned, ready to serve	240g	8 fl oz	1056
Oxtail, low-calorie, canned	240g	8 fl oz	1248
Oxtail, dried, as served	240g	8 fl oz	960
Pea & Ham, canned, ready to serve	240g	8 fl oz	1152
Scotch Broth, canned, ready to serve	240g	8 fl oz	1608
Tomato, Cream of, canned, ready to serve	240g	8 fl oz	1104
Tomato, condensed, canned, as served	240g	8 fl oz	984
Tomato, dried, as served	240g	8 fl oz	936
Vegetable, canned, ready to serve	240g	8 fl oz	1248
Vegetable, low-sodium, dried, as served	240g	8 fl oz	20
Vegetable, low-calorie, canned	240g	8 fl oz	1512
Vegetable, Spring, concentrated, as served	240g	8 fl oz	1306
Vegetable and Beef, low-calorie, canned	240g	8 fl oz	1248
SUGARS:			
Honey	20g	1 tbsp	2
Glucose, liquid	100g	3½ oz	150
Sugar, Demerara	100g	3½ oz	6
white	100g	3½ oz	Tr.
Syrup, golden	20g	1 tbsp	54
maple, pure	20g	1 tbsp	1
maple, imitation	20g	1 tbsp	20
Treacle, black	20g	1 tbsp	19

Food or Drink	Quantity	Approx. portion	Sodium (mg)
SWEETS:			
Boiled sweets	25g	1 oz	6
Butterscotch	25g	1 oz	175
Chewing gum	25g	1 oz	Tr.
Chocolate,			
milk	25g	1 oz	30
plain	25g	1 oz	3
fancy and filled, mixed	25g	1 oz	15
Bounty bar	25g	1 oz	45
Mars bar	25g	1 oz	37
Fruit gums	25g	1 oz	16
Liquorice Allsorts	25g	1 oz	19
Marzipan	25g	1 oz	3
Mints, Glacier	25g	1 oz	9
Nougat	25g	1 oz	16
Pastilles	25g	1 oz	19
Peppermints	25g	1 oz	2
Toffees, mixed	25g	1 oz	80
VEGETABLES:			
Ackee, canned	100g	3½ oz	240
Artichokes, globe, boiled	120g	1 medium	18
Jerusalem, boiled	100g	3½ oz	3
Asparagus, boiled	80g	4 spears	2
canned (average)	80g	4 spears	240
Aubergine	100g	3½ oz	3
Beans,			
baked, canned in tomato sauce	100g	3½ oz	480
broad, boiled	100g	3½ oz	20
canned	100g	3½ oz	270
frozen	100g	3½ oz	3

Food or Drink	Quantity	Approx. portion	Sodium (mg)
VEGETABLES (continued):			
butter, boiled	100g	3½ oz	16
canned	100g	3½ oz	276
dried	100g	3½ oz	62
French, boiled	100g	3½ oz	3
canned	100g	3½ oz	392
frozen	100g	3½ oz	5
haricot, boiled	100g	3½ oz	15
dried	100g	3½ oz	43
Mung, raw	100g	3½ oz	28
red kidney, dried	100g	3½ oz	40
runner, fresh or frozen	100g	3½ oz	2
Bean sprouts, canned	100g	3½ oz	80
Beetroot, boiled	100g	3½ oz	64
Broccoli, raw or frozen	150g	1 stalk	18
boiled	150g	1 stalk	9
Brussels sprouts, boiled	100g	5 medium	2
Cabbage,			
red, raw	100g	3½ oz	32
red, pickled, commercial	25g	1 oz	212
Savoy, boiled	100g	3½ oz	8
spring, boiled	100g	3½ oz	12
white, raw	100g	3½ oz	7
winter, boiled	100g	3½ oz	4
coleslaw, canned, commercial (average)	50g	2 oz	133
coleslaw vinaigrette, commerical (average)	50g	2 oz	153
Carrots, young, boiled	75g	1 carrot	17
canned	100g	3½ oz	280
Cauliflower, raw	100g	3½ oz	8
boiled	100g	3½ oz	4
Celeriac, boiled	100g	3½ oz	28

Food or Drink	Quantity	Approx. portion	Sodium (mg)
VEGETABLES (continued):			
Celery, raw	20g	1 stalk	28
boiled	20g	1 stalk	13
Chicory, raw	100g	3½ oz	7
Courgettes, fresh	100g	3½ oz	Tr.
frozen	100g	3½ oz	20
Cucumber, raw	25g	7 slices	3
Endive, raw	50g	2 oz	5
Horseradish, raw	15g	1 tbsp	1
Horseradish sauce,			
commercial	15g	1 tbsp	60
low-sodium	5g	1 tsp	Tr.
Kohlrabi, boiled	100g	3½ oz	10
Laverbread	100g	3½ oz	560
Leeks, boiled	25g	1 bulb	1
Lentils, raw	100g	3½ oz	36
split, boiled	100g	3½ oz	12
Lettuce, raw	100g	3½ oz	9
Marrow, boiled	100g	3½ oz	1
Mushrooms, raw	50g	2 oz	4
fried	50g	2 oz	5
canned	50g	2 oz	216
Mustard and cress, raw	50g	2 oz	10
Okra, raw	100g	10 pods	7
Onions,			
raw	100g	1 medium	10
boiled	100g	1 medium	7
fried	100g	1 medium	20
pickled	25g	1 onion	175
silverskin	15g	1 onion	131
spring, raw	25g	2 medium	3
Parsley, fresh	25g	1 oz	8
Parsnips, boiled	100g	3½ oz	4

Food or Drink	Quantity	Approx. portion	Sodium (mg)
VEGETABLES (continued):			
Peas,			
fresh, raw	100g	3½ oz	1
boiled	100g	3½ oz	Tr.
frozen, boiled	100g	3½ oz	2
canned, garden	100g	3½ oz	230
mushy	100g	3½ oz	330
processed	100g	3½ oz	330
dried, raw	100g	3½ oz	38
boiled	100g	3½ oz	13
split, dried, raw	100g	3½ oz	38
boiled	100g	3½ oz	14
chick, raw	100g	3½ oz	40
red pigeon, raw	100g	3½ oz	29
Peppers, green, raw	75g	1 pepper	2
Plantain, green, boiled	100g	1 plantain	4
ripe, fried	100g	1 plantain	3
Potatoes,			
old, boiled	150g	1 medium	5
baked	150g	1 medium	9
roast	150g	1 medium	13
new, boiled	100g	1 medium	41
canned	100g	3½ oz	260
chips, fried	50g	10 chips	6
frozen, fried	50g	10 chips	17
crisps, mixed plain and flavoured	20g	10 crisps	110
instant powder(average)	100g	3½ oz	1190
instant, made up	100g	3½ oz	260
salad, canned, commercial	100g	3½ oz	480
Pumpkin, raw	100g	3½ oz	1
cooked, canned	100g	3½ oz	5
Radishes, raw	25g	4 medium	15

Food or Drink	Quantity	Approx. portion	Sodium (mg)
VEGETABLES (continued):			
Salsify, boiled	100g	3½ oz	8
Seakale, boiled	100g	3½ oz	4
Soyabeans, cooked	100g	3½ oz	2
Soyabean curd (tofu)	100g	3½ oz	7
fermented (miso), red	100g	3½ oz	5150
white	100g	3½ oz	3173
Spinach, fresh, boiled	100g	3½ oz	120
frozen	100g	3½ oz	57
canned	100g	3½ oz	338
Spring greens, boiled	100g	3½ oz	10
Swedes, raw	100g	3½ oz	52
boiled	100g	3½ oz	14
Sweetcorn, boiled	140g	1 cob	1
kernels, canned, commercial (average)	100g	3½ oz	310
Sweet potatoes, boiled	130g	1 potato	23
Tomatoes, raw or fried	125g	1 tomato	4
canned	100g	3½ oz	29
Tomato juice, canned	100ml	4 fl oz	240
Tomato purée	25g	1 oz	105
unsalted	25g	1 oz	5
Tomato cooking sauce	100g	3½ oz	850
Turnips, boiled	100g	3½ oz	28
Turnip tops, boiled	100g	3½ oz	7
Vegetables, mixed, canned	100g	3½ oz	306
frozen	100g	3½ oz	58
Vegetable salad, canned	100g	3½ oz	440
Watercress	50g	2 oz	30
Yams, boiled	100g	3½ oz	17

Food or Drink	Quantity	Approx. portion	Sodium (mg)
MISCELLANEOUS:			
Baking powder, standard (average)	3g	1 tsp	354
low-sodium	3g	1 tsp	Tr.
Bicarbonate of soda	3g	1 tsp	822
Cream of tartar	3g	1 tsp	Tr.
Meat tenderizer, commercial	5g	1 tsp	1953
M.S.G. (monosodium glutamate)	5g	1 tsp	680
Potassium glutamate (M.S.G. substitute)	5g	1 tsp	Tr.
Saccharin (Hermesetas)	5g	1 tablet	2
Yeast, baker's compressed	25g	1 oz	4
dried	25g	1 oz	12

Appendix II
Herb and Spice Chart

Herb or Spice	How it is available	Sodium mg/tsp	How to use it
Allspice	whole or ground	1.4	With many main dishes. In juices, soups, spicy sauces. With peas, spinach, turnips and red and yellow vegetables.
Anise	whole or ground	N/A	In fruit pies and fillings. With carrots, beetroot, cottage cheese.
Basil, sweet	fresh, whole or ground	0.4	With eggs, soups, sauces, salads, tomato dishes, rice, most vegetables. In fruit compotes.
Bay leaf	whole leaves, dried or ground	0.3	With sauces, stews, pickled vegetables and in gravies.
Caraway	whole seed or ground	0.4	With beans, beetroot, soups, in breads and biscuits, in casseroles and home-made cheese spreads.

Herb or Spice	How it is available	Sodium mg/tsp.	How to use it
Cardamom	whole seed or ground	0.2	In pies and pastries, biscuits, fruit dishes and pumpkin pie.
Cayenne	ground	N/A	Use very sparingly since it's a hot blend. With casseroles, soups, curries and vegetables.
Celery seed	whole or ground	4.1	In soups, coleslaw, with cauliflower, asparagus, and in herbed breads.
Chervil	fresh or whole	N/A	In soups and salads, garnishes, cooked dishes, eggs, sauces and dressings for vegetables.
Chilli powder	powder	0.2	Often a blend of dried chillies, cumin, garlic and onion powder. Some brands may include salt. Use sparingly, according to strength, in soups, egg dishes and dressings.
Chives	fresh, frozen or dried	N/A	As a garnish, or to accent flavour, with cooked dishes, vegetables, cheese and in salads.

Herb or Spice	How it is available	Sodium mg/tsp.	How to use it
Cinnamon	whole sticks or ground	0.2	In pastries and puddings, with fruits, spicy dishes and drinks, carrots and sweet potatoes.
Cloves	whole or ground	4.2	Use sparingly as it can be penetrating and pungent. With fruits, puddings and pies, in soups, sauces, bean dishes and carrots.
Coriander	whole seed or ground	0.3	In pastry, biscuits, soups, salads and dressings. Enhances baked apples or apple-sauce.
	leaves	N/A	Use as you would parsley.
Cumin	ground or seed	2.6	In cooked dishes, devilled eggs, soups, rice and in fruit pies.
Curry	powder	1.0	A blend of many spices, the strength and pungency can vary according to blend and brand. With savoury dishes, vegetables, fruits, cream cheese. Some blends may contain salt.

Herb or Spice	How it is available	Sodium mg/tsp	How to use it
Dill	fresh leaves, whole or ground, or seed	0.2	With soups and chowders. With cooked dishes, in dressings and potato salad.
Fennel	whole or ground, or seed	1.9	In breads, sweet pastries and biscuits. With many dishes, including eggs, beetroot, cabbage and apple dishes.
Fenugreek	ground or seed	N/A	In curries, sauces, soups, and used in making imitation vanilla flavouring.
Garlic	fresh bulbs or dried, powder or minced	0.1	With many savoury dishes, vegetables, breads, soups and salad dressings.
Ginger	fresh whole root, powder, or crystallized	0.5	In biscuits, cakes, pies, chutneys and pickles, curry, and spicy drinks. With yellow and red vegetables.
Mace	whole or ground	1.3	With yellow vegetables, in biscuits and puddings or as a garnish.

Herb and Spice Chart

Herb or Spice	How it is available	Sodium mg/tsp	How to use it
Marjoram	fresh, whole, or ground	1.3	With cooked dishes, soups, egg dishes, many vegetables and in sauces.
Mint	fresh leaves or dried	N/A	With lamb, fish, soups and sauces, and many vegetables.
Mustard	whole seed or ground	0.1	With many cooked dishes, soups, dressings and many vegetables.
Nutmeg	whole seed or ground	0.2	In many puddings, sauces and soups, and with many vegetables and fruits.
Onion powder	ground	0.8	In most savoury dishes, dressings and sauces, and with most vegetables.
Oregano (wild marjoram)	fresh, whole or ground	0.3	With savoury main dishes, egg dishes, pasta, vegetables, and salads.
Paprika	ground	0.4	With poultry, goulash, soups and on coleslaw. As a garnish or as an ingredient.

Herb or Spice	How it is available	Sodium mg/tsp	How to use it
Parsley	fresh or dried flakes	5.9	Garnishing dishes or as an ingredient. In soups, main courses, many vegetables, egg dishes, salads and dumplings.
Pepper, black, red or white	whole or ground	0.2	As an ingredient or as a garnish. For all savoury dishes, and also gingerbreads.
Poppy seed	whole dried seeds	0.2	For garnishing dishes or as an ingredient. On breads, biscuits, cakes, in soups, pasta dishes, with many vegetables, cottage cheese, and in stuffings.
Rosemary	fresh or whole, ground	0.5	Can be pungent, so use cautiously. With main courses, soups, egg dishes, herb breads, marinades, barbecue sauce and dressings.
Saffron	whole or ground	2.0	Very expensive, but a small amount has a great effect, adding colour and a bitter-sweet flavour. For rice, potatoes, breads, chowders, curries, egg dishes and cakes.

Herb or Spice	How it is available	Sodium mg/tsp	How to use it
Sage	fresh, whole or ground	0.1	Use cautiously as it can be pungent. With savoury dishes, in chowders, consommé and gravies, with salads, many vegetables and pasta.
Savory	fresh, whole or ground	0.3	In soups and main dishes, as you would use sage. With rice dishes, many vegetables and in stuffings.
Sesame	whole seed	0.6	In breads, biscuits and sweet rolls. As a garnish or an ingredient, with vegetables, casseroles, pasta and on salads.
Tarragon	fresh, whole or ground	1.0	In egg dishes, light main courses, chowders, herb butters, vinegars and many vegetables.
Thyme	fresh, whole or ground	1.2	With many dishes, soups and aspics, egg dishes and many vegetables.

Herb or Spice	How it is available	Sodium mg/tsp	How to use it
Turmeric	whole or ground	0.2	Can substitute for the more expensive saffron. Use for a golden colour in creamed soups, chowders, curries, rice, many vegetables, and breads.
Watercress	fresh leaves	3.0	As a garnish or as an ingredient. In salads, fruit cocktails, soups, egg dishes, and with many main courses.

(Sodium values are by courtesy of the American Spice Trade Association)

Appendix III

Low-Sodium Food Manufacturers

Del Monte Foods Ltd.
Astronaut House
Hounslow Road
Feltham
Middlesex TW14 9AE.

'No-salt-added' canned carrots, green beans, peas, sweetcorn.

Ener-G Foods, Inc
6901 Fox Avenue South
P.O. Box 24723
Seattle, Washington
98124-0723, USA.

(Imported) Low-sodium flours, cereals, cookies, baking powder and sodium-free salt-substitutes.

G.F. Dietary Supplies Ltd
Lowther Road
Stanmore
Middlesex HA7 1EL.

Unsalted rice cakes, low-sodium wafer-biscuits and pasta products (imported from Italy and U.S.A).

Gilbert's Health Foods Ltd
37 Swinegate
Grantham
Lincs NG31 6RN.

Sodium-free and reduced-sodium salt-substitutes.

Hain Pure Food Co.
13660 So. Figueroa
Los Angeles, California
90061, USA.

(Imported) Unsalted mayonnaise, dressings, nut butters, soups, juices, margarine, condiments and crackers.

Health & Diet Food Co. Ltd Seymour House South Street Godalming Surrey GU7 1BZ.	Low-sodium soups (imported from *Hugli Foods*, Switzerland).
Health Valley Foods 700 Union Street Montebello, California 90640, USA.	(Imported) Many reduced-sodium foods including 'no-salt-added' soups and breakfast cereals.
Klinge Chemicals Ltd 7 Albion Way Kelvin Industrial Estate E. Kilbride Lanarkshire G75 0SL	*Lo Salt* low-sodium salt-substitute.
Larkhall Laboratories (*Cantassium*) 225-229 Putney Bridge Road London SW15 2PY.	*Trufree* sodium-free salt-substitute, *Ruthmol* low-sodium salt, *Salfree* baking powder, and low-sodium bran cereals.
Lawry's Foods, Inc. 570 West Avenue 26 Los Angeles, California 90065, USA.	(Imported) Seasoned pepper.
McCormick & Co. 414 Light Street Baltimore, Maryland 21202, USA.	(Imported) Low-sodium salt-substitutes, spices and herbs.
Modern Products, Inc. P.O. Box 09398 Milwaukee, Wisconsin 53209, USA.	(Imported) *Vegit, Santay, Onion Magic,* and *Herbal Bouquet* spices, herbs and salt-substitutes.

Low-Sodium Food Manufacturers

Prewett's Stone Flour Mills
Horsham, Surrey.

Prewett's low-sodium salt-substitute.

RHM Foods Limited
Wythenshawe
Manchester M22 7AH.

Cerebos Mineral low-sodium salt-substitute.

I. *Rokeach & Sons, Inc.*
560 Sylvan Avenue
Englewood Cliffs
New Jersey
07632, U.S.A.

Unsalted borscht soup (imported for Passover season only).

St. Giles Foods Ltd
(Meridien Foods Ltd)
St Giles House
Sandhurst Road
Sidcup, Kent DA15 7HL.

Life brand low-sodium tomato ketchup, brown sauce, mustards, Worcestershire sauce, salad cream, mayonnaise, tartar sauce, and horseradish sauce. Also larger-size catering packs of low-sodium soups.

Welfare Foods Ltd
London Road South
Poynton
Stockport SK12 1LA.

Rite-Diet low-sodium canned bread, low-sodium biscuits, flours, and pasta.

Index

analgesics, 67, 68-69
anchovies, 27, 56
antacids, 13, 67
apples, 45, 92
arteries, 16
aspirin, 68

baby food, 31
bacon, 26, 45, 50, 56, 95
baked beans, 45, 59, 106
baker's salt, enriched, 24
baking powder, 28, 34, 36, 45, 111
baking soda, *see* Bicarbonate of soda
bananas, 45, 92
beef, 46, 95
  stock cubes, 37, 50, 80
beers, 13, 65, 79
beverages, 61-65, 79
bicarbonate of soda
  as toothpaste, 68
  in foods, 14, 27, 34, 36, 46
  in medicines, 67, 68
  sodium content of, 111
  with vegetables, 45, 50
biscuits, 46, 57, 83
black pudding, 26, 96
blood-pressure, 13-17, 20, 31-32
breads, 13, 27, 35, 46, 58, 83

breakfast cereals, 13, 27, 35, 47, 56, 84
brines, 20, 21, 27, 34
butter, 36, 85

cabbage, 42, 107
cakes, 27, 47, 57, 85
cancer, 12, 18
canning salt, 24
canteens, 55-56
cheese, 26, 35-36, 47, 57, 58, 85
chicken, 47, 57, 100
chloride, 14, 38
chocolate, 48, 54, 65, 106
cholesterol, 56, 72
chutney, 48, 52
cocoa, 48, 64, 82
coffee, 48, 64, 80
computers, 71-78
condiments, 48, 102
contraceptive pills, 17
corned beef, 26, 46, 95, 98
cornish pasties, 26, 52, 98
courgettes, 54, 58
crackers, 46, 83
cream, 86
crispbreads, 46, 57, 58, 83
crisps, 13, 20, 27, 35, 52, 53
custard sauce, 48

dairy products, 65, 85
de-icing salt, 24
delicatessens, 55, 57
denture cleaners, 68
  fixatives, 68
desserts, 48, 101
diabetes, 12, 69
distilled water, 58, 62
diuretics, 18, 31
dried fruits, 28, 49

eggs, 46, 49, 56, 58, 87
E numbers, 29, 34
evaporated salt, 24
exercise, 17, 19, 72, 73

fats, 12, 17, 49, 65, 72, 88
fish, 26-27, 33, 49, 58, 88
fish cakes, 49, 88
flour, 47, 48, 52, 91
flour salt, 25
frankfurters, 49
french dressing, 51, 102
fruit juices, 50
fruits, 46, 48, 50, 57, 59, 92-95
  dried, 28, 49

game, 100
Garden Blend, 42
gargles, 68
garlic, 51, 116
garlic powder, 37
garlic salt, 37, 56, 103
gelatine, 50
Grandma's Herbs, 42
gravy and gravy mixes, 35, 50, 56, 102

halite, 21, 25
ham, 13, 26, 50, 56, 97
heart attacks, 15, 20

herb vinegars, 42
herbs, 33, 37, 38-43, 49, 51, 113-120
hypertension, 11, 15-16, 31, 65, 72

ice-cream, 25, 101
ice-cream salt, 25
indigestion remedies, 68-69
iodized salt, 25

jams, 50, 101
jellies, 48, 50, 57, 101

kidneys, 13, 14, 16, 17-18, 31, 38
kippers, 27, 49, 89
kosher salt, 25

labelling, 34
lamb, 50, 96
laverbread, 38, 108
laxatives, 13, 67, 69
lemonade, 64, 80
lemons, 37, 43-44, 48, 53, 93
low-sodium food manufacturers, 121
luncheon meats, 26, 56, 98

MSG *see* monosodium glutamate
macaroni, 53, 91
margarines, 36, 48, 54, 56, 88
matzohs, 46, 57, 58, 83
mayonnaise, 51, 53, 58, 102
meat, 26, 33, 36, 57, 95-98
meat tenderizers, 37, 111
medicines, 67
menopause, 18
milk, 26, 64, 82
mineral waters, 62
monosodium glutamate, 14, 27, 34, 56, 111
mouthwashes, 68

mustards, 37, 48, 102

nuts, 13, 20, 51, 53, 99

oedema, 17
oestrogen, 17-18
oils, 88
olives, 27, 53, 56, 57, 94, 102
onion powder, 37
onion salt, 37, 56, 103
onions, 49, 51, 58, 65, 102, 108
oranges, 48, 94

pancake syrup, 51
pancakes, 51
pasta, 53, 91, 92
peaches, 45, 94
peanut butter, 51, 59, 101
peanuts, 99
pears, 45, 94
peas, 13, 52, 109
pepper, 39, 102
pickles, 27, 37, 48, 52, 57, 102
picnics, 58-59
pies, 26, 43, 46, 52, 57
plums, 45, 94
popcorn, 53
popcorn salt, 25
pork, 52, 97
potassium, 13, 18, 38, 45, 46, 72
potatoes, 43, 52, 109
poultry, 26, 33, 36, 100
pregnancy, 18
premenstrual symptoms, 17
pretzel salt, 25
pretzels, 53
progesterone, 17
puddings, 27, 48, 101

renin, 14
restaurants, 55-56

rice, 43, 53, 91
rock salt, 23, 25, 37

saccharin, 28, 50, 64, 67, 68, 111
salad cream, 53, 56, 57, 103
salad dressing, 37, 53
salads, 53, 56, 57
salt
  cellars, 19, 22, 33, 37
  deposits, 21-23
  history of, 21-23
  production of, 23-24
  requirements, 30
  substitutes, 38, 103
  tablets, 30
  taxes, 22
sandwich fillings, 58-59
sauces, 48, 52, 56, 102
sausages, 26, 46, 49, 56, 57, 97
sea lettuce, 38
sea salt, 23, 25, 37
sea-water, 21, 25, 32, 61
seaweed, 31, 38
shellfish, 49, 90
smoking, 17
snacks, 20, 31, 51, 53
soda water, 64, 81
sodium
  compounds, 11, 14, 26-28, 36, 67
  requirements, 30
sodium-free baking powder, 45
soft drinks, 31, 64, 80
software for computers, 71-78
solar salt, 25
soups, 27, 53, 56, 59, 104-105
soya sauce, 34, 37, 43, 48, 56, 103
spaghetti, 45, 53, 92
spices, 33, 38, 51
spirits, 65, 79

strawberries, 18, 46, 59, 95
stress, 17
strokes, 15, 16, 20, 31
stuffings, 47, 54
suet, 49, 88
sugars, 105
sweets, 54, 106
syrup, golden, 50, 51, 101
  maple, 51, 101

tea, 48, 64, 80
tomatoes, 43, 45, 53-54, 110
tomato juice, 56, 64, 81, 110
  ketchup, 54, 103
  paste (purée), 54, 110
tonic water, 64, 81
toothpastes, 13, 68
trace mineralized salt, 25
treacle, black, 50, 51, 101

tuna, 26, 49, 58, 90
turkey, 54, 57, 100

vegetables, 33, 36, 42-43, 50, 52, 106
vinegar, 50, 51, 52, 56, 103
vitamins, 14, 70, 72

water, 19, 26, 33, 58, 61, 65
water retention, 17, 19
water softener salt, 26
wines, 51, 65, 79
Worcestershire sauce, 37, 43, 48, 103

yogurt, 36, 58, 87

zucchini *see* courgettes